D0380861

EFFECTIVE
Teacher Hiring

A Guide
to Getting
the Best

Kenneth D. Peterson

ASSOCIATION FOR SUPERVISION
AND CURRICULUM DEVELOPMENT
ALEXANDRIA, VIRGINIA USA

Association for Supervision and Curriculum Development
1703 N. Beauregard St. • Alexandria, VA 22311-1714 USA
Telephone: 1-800-933-2723 or 703-578-9600 • Fax: 703-575-5400
Web site: http://www.ascd.org • E-mail: member@ascd.org

ASCD publications present a variety of viewpoints. The views expressed or implied in this book should not be interpreted as official positions of the Association.

All Web links in this book are correct as of the publication date below but may have become inactive or otherwise modified since that time. If you notice a deactivated or changed link, please e-mail books@ascd.org with the words "Link Update" in the subject line. In your message, please specify the Web link, the book title, and the page number on which the link appears.

Printed in the United States of America.

S10/2002

ASCD Product No. 102047
ASCD member price: $18.95   nonmember price: $22.95

Library of Congress Cataloging-in-Publication Data

Peterson, Kenneth D.
  Effective teacher hiring : a guide to getting the best / Kenneth D.
Peterson.
      p. cm.
Includes bibliographical references (p.   ) and index.
  ISBN 0-87120-675-7 (alk. paper)
  1. Teachers—Selection and appointment—United States. I. Title.
  LB2835.25 .P48 2002
  331.7'6113711'00973—dc21
                              2002009500

11 10 09 08 07 06 05 04 03 02   10 9 8 7 6 5 4 3 2 1

EFFECTIVE TEACHER HIRING: A GUIDE TO GETTING THE BEST

ACKNOWLEDGMENTS

Thanks to Bob Cole and Ernesto Yermoli for their help with the manuscript. I would also like to extend my appreciation to the scholars who preceded me in this topic: Barnett Berry, Dale Bolton, Linda Darling-Hammond, Michael Scriven, and Arthur Wise. Additional thanks to Judith Cunningham, Maggie Hewitt, Dave Kassler, Krista McCleary, Kathy Narramore, Rich Ponzio, Barbara Ruben, Cliff York, and one dear anonymous friend for their personal support. Additional thanks to Bonnie, Cathy, Rudi, Jenna, and Ben.

I have been a preservice teacher educator for 30 years in California, Utah, and Oregon; this book is dedicated to the student teachers I came to know in those places.

Teacher hiring is a time of renewing, energizing, and restoring hope. My wish is that this book helps us to recall why we are educators.

INTRODUCTION

I wrote this book because no single school-district activity beyond the moment-to-moment care of young people is more important than the hiring of talented, accomplished, and effective teachers. New efforts at reforming schools, closing racial achievement gaps, increasing academic performance, and building curriculum all rely on teachers who can grasp the issues and help develop solutions. Seventy years ago, Graces wrote that "wise selection is the best means of improving the [educational] system, and the greatest lack of economy exists whenever teachers have been poorly chosen" (1932, p. 191). More recently, Black and English said that the "only lasting mark any administrator can make . . . is the quality of staff he or she hires" (1986, p. 171).

Unfortunately, there is currently relatively little research about teacher selection available. Not much has changed since 1977, when E. S. Stanton noted that, "with the exception of the conceptual model of [future prediction performance], not a single scientific hypothesis or theory related to performance prediction has consistently withstood the test of empirical and investigative scrutiny" (p. 103). Established teacher-selection procedures that might serve as models to other schools and districts are scarce as well. Outstanding hiring systems are often due as much to a serendipitous combination of geography, economics, and remarkably strong educator leadership as to a particular hiring blueprint. While the influence of such ancillary factors cannot be denied, the procedures outlined in this book, if properly implemented, will ensure a superior selection process regardless of a district's location or budget.

Six Principles of Good Teacher Hiring

It's worth the effort to hire the best. Hiring the best possible candidates makes a long-term difference to school-district quality. By increasing student learning, good teachers gradually improve any district, and often help improve their fellow teachers as well.

Good hiring requires a complicated selection system. Good teacher hiring should be done in stages, involving various people in separate roles and employing a variety of information sources. Although track records are the best predictors of future success, most teacher candidates are beginners with limited professional histories; additional criteria, such as interviews and recommendations, should therefore be thoughtfully considered when assessing first-time applicants.

Some people hire better than others. Not everyone who wants to hire teachers is good at it; managing, supervising, and hiring are distinctly different administrative activities. The best indicator of a good hirer is a solid hiring track record.

A fair and lawful selection system is vital. Educators have a moral duty to treat people well. Federal, state and local laws must be followed at all times, and the biases inherent in critical discernment must be controlled.

Teacher hiring must be tied in with school district planning. The vision for teacher hiring should extend beyond the immediate vacancy. It should include needs analysis, strategic planning, environmental scans, goal setting, visioning, projections, mission examination, and thinking about the setting, in addition to the facts of the current opening and need.

Teacher selectors must sell their districts or schools. Good hirers must clearly emphasize the most attractive aspects of their schools or districts. They should also know what schools or districts their best current teachers came from, as well as why they chose to relocate.

Teacher selection works best when it is approached in a rational, organized manner. Though current research does not spell out all we would like to know about hiring, the strategies and techniques provided in this book can help mobilize you to hire the best teachers from the largest possible pools of candidates.

PRELIMINARY PROCEDURES

How *Not* to Hire a Teacher

In order to implement effective school hiring procedures, we first must identify the characteristics of poor hiring. The teacher-selection practice at many schools and districts suffers from poorly conceived recruitment systems, limited applicant pools, and poor training on the part of recruiters. Wise, Darling-Hammond, and Berry (1988) have also identified limited recruitment, overly narrow bases for applicant screening, and disorganization regarding paperwork, communication, and timing as common errors. The following vignettes provide examples of bad hiring in action; each exhibits at least a few of the typical hiring mistakes listed in Figure 1.1.

Vignette #1

The district office sends Principal Paul Edwards the application files of three potential social studies teachers who were screened and interviewed at the central office. The group contains an outstanding basketball coach, Bill DeBry, who used to be the assistant coach of a nearby team for inner-city young women. Mr. DeBry's recommendations are strong—all of them mention his popularity with students— and he is a dynamic interviewee, suggesting ideas for more efficient

1.1
The Most Common Teacher-Hiring Mistakes

☞ Insufficient time allotted to recruitment.

☞ Too small a pool of applicants.

☞ Wrong people doing the hiring, chosen regardless of recruitment track record.

☞ Hirers not trained, mentored, monitored, or evaluated.

☞ Reliance on limited recruitment sources (e.g., friends, neighbors, relatives, student teachers, substitutes).

☞ Narrow hiring criteria (e.g., adequate grade level, subject); less obvious but equally important attributes (e.g., flexibility, diversity) ignored.

☞ Hiring limited to immediate vacancies only.

☞ Hiring not tied into district's long-term planning efforts.

☞ Best objective evidence on candidate quality, such as references from professors or test scores, not sought.

☞ Failure to emphasize (or even to use) academic criteria, such as test scores or course grades.

☞ Failure to adequately assess applicant's work with students (decision based solely on adult approval of candidate).

☞ Overreliance on interviews.

☞ Hiring of athletic coaches with only nominal classroom aptitude due to school or district pressure.

☞ Hiring based on physical appearance of applicant.

☞ Disregard of applicant's growth potential.

☞ Hiring criteria unrelated to job or performance.

☞ Emphasis on a particular style, method, or technique of teaching.

☞ Eliminating candidates who don't meet all criteria, without considering their overall comparative competence.

☞ Procedures, policies, or patterns of hiring discriminate against certain groups of candidates.

☞ Disregard of candidate's demonstrated effect on student achievement.

☞ Hirer prejudices left unchecked.

☞ Selection criteria not examined or discussed in public.

☞ All interested parties not involved in hiring.

☞ Inadequate check of candidate materials for accuracy or honesty.

☞ Inadequate follow-up on those providing recommendations for credibility and additional information.

☞ Candidates asked unfair or illegal questions.

☞ Applicant privacy violated.

☞ Advantages and strengths of hiring district inadequately conveyed during recruitment.

☞ Selection system not evaluated after each round of hiring.

team teaching and offering his extensive library of history videos for use in the classroom.

Mr. Edwards selects Mr. DeBry on the strength of his qualifications, without considering the other two candidates.

"He is an excellent social studies teacher, and a winning personality," says Mr. Edwards. "Also, he will develop our young women's basketball program. This school needs community recognition; our test scores are middling, and our funding and morale are low. Sports teams stand strong in this community."

What's the problem? *Mr. Edwards has ignored the quality of work among Mr. DeBry's students, and has focused on the candidate's contribution to athletics, when the open position is for social studies.*

Vignette #2

"In this district we place a heavy emphasis on school-improvement management," says the superintendent to applicant Lisa Sandholtz. "I see you attended the after-school planning meetings at the school where you student-taught. How much do you know about local school planning? If you were hired to fill this position, would you continue to participate fully?"

"Well," says Lisa, "I feel that I have both a theoretical and practical understanding of school improvement. As you can see from my portfolio, I carried out parent surveys with my cooperating teacher. We found that parents wanted more homework and a Web site for updates on classroom assignments. I feel that school-improvement programs really help teacher morale."

The superintendent sits back in her chair.

"Lisa, you were the only candidate for this position with experience in school improvement. As you know, by having teachers work as partners with parents and principals on local problems, we get school-wide progress. Personally, I know that this type of group effort works better than other kinds of school reform, such as more testing and standards. We need teachers who will put in extra planning time with each other here in our district. I think you'll be a fine addition to our district."

What's the problem? *The superintendent has focused on a single narrow hiring criterion—school-improvement management. In addition, he has not involved the judgment of Lisa's own teachers or consulted with others before making his selection.*

Vignette #3

Dr. Schwartz calls a professor at the local teacher-education program, who strongly recommends a recent applicant, describing her as one of the top five in a large group of talented student teachers. After selecting one more promising application from the district office, Dr. Schwartz interviews both candidates. She calls a teacher to sit in on the second half of one candidate's interview. In the end, the applicant recommended by the university is offered the job.

What's the problem? *Dr. Schwartz has chosen from too small a pool of candidates and has inconsistently considered the perspectives of current faculty. Like the superintendents in the other two vignettes, he has attached too much importance to information gleaned from interviews.*

Effects of Bad Hiring

The quality of new hires affects not only the students but also community opinion, school morale, and the burdens of veteran teachers. Teacher dismissal due to poor hiring threatens program continuity and parent and student support, and intimidates the other instructors. It's expensive, too: Bridges (1992) estimates that it costs school districts between $50,000 and $100,000 to dismiss a teacher. As Bolton (1973) has noted, "the cost of hiring the wrong candidates can be higher in terms of supplementary training, wasted salary, adverse public relations, and lost productivity than the cost of more extensive recruitment" (p. 10). Yet despite the high stakes, most school districts allocate few resources to teacher hiring. Experts on personnel management estimate that school districts spend 8 percent of what business and industry invest in employee recruitment (Bolton, 1973).

Assumptions and Hiring Variables

Teacher hiring is often more complicated than are the practices discussed in this book, and districts and school practices vary depending on the resources available. Some districts, for instance, might contain large pools of qualified applicants, while others must seek candidates out of state. I make the assumption in this book that districts have reasonably large applicant pools to choose from.

Principal Participation

Though principals are often the best judges and mediators in the hiring process, they can also undermine the district by attending only to the needs of their school. For example, principals may keep information about candidate availability from the central office until their favorite prospects qualify for interviews. Principals can also forward the names of applicants they would like to hire to the central office, thereby providing favored applicants with an unfair advantage over the rest.

Teacher Participation

Another variable in the hiring process is the degree of teacher participation, which is essential. Teachers can provide insight into the day-to-day reality of classroom practice—thereby balancing the perspectives of other district personnel—and teachers who participate in hiring are likelier to support both their new colleagues and the hiring process itself. On the other hand, including more participants in the selection process can also heighten the level of gossip and, consequently, may impede confidentiality.

Centralization vs. School-Led Selection

Teacher hiring can either be centralized at the district office or conducted independently by each school. The views and needs of these locations differ greatly, thereby affecting the selection process. For example, some schools might not understand the time demands of central screening procedures, which can frustrate and discourage applicants.

Creating a Teacher Selection System

A valid teacher selection system should
- Include specific, clearly delineated selection criteria
- Fit into a larger conceptual scheme of good education
- Be agreed upon by local teachers, administrators, and personnel-selection researchers
- Not leave out important ideas about teaching and learning
- Attempt to predict good teaching
- Reliably document and use candidate information
- Compare favorably with other district hiring systems
- Preclude negative side effects, such as the exclusion of particular teaching styles

Committing to the Task

A successful district must agree on the importance of effective teacher selection, and all participants in the process must be strongly committed to the task. School-board members must say that they want the best teachers, superintendents should publicly emphasize the priority of good hiring, teachers should call for the best colleagues, parents should voice their preferences, and administrators should provide as much of their time as is necessary.

The district should consider district goals when discussing the need for new teachers: strong classroom performers, teachers who meet student needs and priorities, visible gains among different types of learning, and flexible innovators who adapt to change and respond to challenges. Different groups—that is, teachers, board members, and administrators—should initiate these discussions among themselves and with each other. The district should recognize that upset feelings and temporary disturbances are a regular part of the hiring process—such as when some teachers are asked to contribute, but not others—and may want to adopt a set of principles of good hiring, such as in Figure 1.2. Finally, the district should elucidate its most outstanding qualities: current best practices, remarkable results, and common ideals. Specific district values should be affirmed early in the hiring process.

Finding the Finders

Selecting the hirers is one of the most difficult and important preparation tasks of the selection process. Many of us think of ourselves as able to judge the quality of teachers, but in practice, not all of us hire well. A good hirer will have a track record of successful past selections, regardless of her role or even of the quality of her own work.

Ensuring Legal Compliance

Given the sensitive nature of the information collected during the hiring process, the district or school should consult an attorney for guidance during the system design phase. Once the system is ready to be implemented, it should be thoroughly reviewed by a lawyer. A

1.2
Guiding Principles of a Teacher-Hiring System

The teacher-hiring system should
- ☞ Conform to legal requirements of personnel selection and hiring
- ☞ Be understood and valued by district personnel, the school board, and the community
- ☞ Secure the best possible educators and meet district needs
- ☞ Be based upon the best objective evidence available
- ☞ Exhibit logical analyses of procedures and decisions
- ☞ Keep biases in check
- ☞ Involve all interested audiences
- ☞ Employ multiple and variable data sources
- ☞ Promote equality of opportunity for student learning by hiring teachers with different characteristics, experiences, and strengths
- ☞ Promote equality of opportunity for professional practice
- ☞ Be based on teacher role expectations derived from national professional standards (National Board for Professional Teaching Standards, 1996)
- ☞ Meet professional standards for sound personnel evaluation, including those of *propriety, utility, feasibility,* and *accuracy* (Joint Committee on Standards for Educational Evaluation, 1988)
- ☞ Support the rights of the candidates, community, and district
- ☞ Emphasize assessment of and assistance for beginning teachers
- ☞ Be subject to evaluation, validation, refinement, and updating

---

personnel advocate lawyer should conduct a one-time review of the entire system, looking specifically for an aggrieved candidate challenge. Finally, the district should create a Teacher Selection Task Force, a Selection Committee, and a Teacher Applicant Screening Team (see Figure 1.3).

Teacher Selection Task Force

The hiring district should create a Teacher Selection Task Force—a standing district committee that recommends hiring policy.

1.3
Teacher Selection Groups

Superintendent
Purpose: Selects or approves members of hiring groups; makes final hiring decisions

Teacher Selection Task Force
Purpose: Recommends hiring policy
Consists of: Administrators, teachers, parents, older students, and community members

Teacher Selection Committee
Purpose: Selecting the new hire
Consists of: Equal number of administrators and teachers, along with assorted clerical staff, parents, older students, and community members

Teacher Applicant Screening Team
Purpose: Screens applicants for eligibility and prepares candidate records
Consists of: An administrator, a teacher, and some clerical assistance

The Task Force would not directly hire teachers, but create the necessary conditions in the district to hire well. The group should consist of administrators, teachers, parents, older students, and community members, and should report to the superintendent. Smaller districts might assemble and share a Task Force with neighboring districts. Duties of the Task Force include

- Initiating hiring workshops
- Designing training
- Securing inservice materials
- Coordinating hiring with the district's strategic plan
- Overseeing selection-process validation studies
- Managing district hiring resources
- Keeping contacts for local teacher-education institutions

Teacher Selection Committee

The Teacher Selection Committee is a group of 8 to 12 people charged with actually selecting the new hire. The Committee's job is to reduce the number of applicants for each position, first to a group of four to six and then to a priority ranking of the top three. Committee members should include the best hirers in their district. Generally, the Committee should consist of equal numbers of administrators and teachers, along with assorted clerical staff, parents, older students, and community members. Members should be nominated by relevant organizations, such as teachers' organizations and PTAs; principals should nominate students, and the superintendent should ultimately select all the members. The Committee must answer to the Task Force and should recommend hirers to the superintendent. The current practice in most districts of involving only volunteer teachers in the hiring process needs to be reappraised, so that the best performing instructors can have a say in selection. At least one of the teacher Committee members should be experienced in the subject area of the open position and should review candidate unit plans, work samples, sample lessons, and student achievement information. The inclusion of even a single student on the Committee allows those who will be most affected by the new hire to make their views known.

The Committee should receive inservice training, both at its inception and on a regular basis thereafter, including readings, role playing, and explication of the selection system. The district might consider an additional stipend for teacher Committee members.

Teacher Applicant Screening Team

The Screening Team screens applicants for eligibility and prepares candidate records. The team should consist of an administrator, a teacher, and some clerical assistants; members should report to and be chosen by the Hiring Task Force. Additional duties of the team include

☛ Scheduling candidate interviews
☛ Allocating resources
☛ Communicating with the other hiring groups
☛ Maintaining the Web site

Final Selection

The superintendent (or a designee) ultimately makes the decision to hire.

Hiring Resource Book

The Selection Committee should create a hiring resource book—including activities, calendars, record-keeping materials, and documentation of each school's hiring history—to use as a hiring guide and learning resource for district personnel.

Trial Run

A trial run of the selection system on several current veteran teachers, who can pretend to be candidates and play-act the hiring process, will disclose further needs for development, and also serve as effective training for the real thing.

Small District Procedures

While large districts can support large staffs and afford a multitude of resources, smaller districts have fewer assets immediately at hand. Consequently, small districts should network with other districts and share tasks and resources with them.

Defining the Position

There are five essential factors to consider when defining the teaching position:

☞ Grade level and subject matter
☞ Necessary interpersonal skills
☞ Community requirements
☞ Cultural, ethnic, and gender diversity
☞ District goals

Immediate needs should be addressed first, but with an eye to future teacher lineups. For example, having a number of primary teachers close to retirement might call for new hires to gain experience for replacement. The characteristics necessary for the position should be derived from a district mission statement and conform to duties statements for teachers in the district, the job description of the specific position, and a school-based needs assessment.

Candidates for the open position should fit the needs of the local community. For example, large family-income differences call for teachers who know how communities handle conflict between the rich and poor.

Different types of teachers require different kinds of interpersonal skills, and the hiring school should have a mix of these to call upon. Encourage hirers to ask teachers, students, and parents about the kinds of teachers they want at the school. You can also acquire this information by having the hirers meet with the district's strategic planners; interviewing the departing teacher; analyzing current top performers in similar positions; and reviewing the policies and strategies of other districts and schools.

Job Descriptions

Job descriptions should include the characteristics of teachers recommended by the Interstate New Teacher Assessment and Support Consortium (1992) and the National Board for Professional Teaching Standards (1996), along with lists of duties as compiled by local teachers. Job descriptions should be simple and direct, and should contain no more than five major functional responsibilities (see Figure 1.4). They are more like working statements than blueprints for exact replication; the job of a teacher is complex and open-ended, and even extensive descriptions can't capture the full nature of the teacher's job.

Recruitment Methods

Although essential to optimal hiring, candidate recruitment is a weakness of most school districts. A teacher-recruitment system should be vigorous, energetic, imaginative, and unique; it must attract as well as inform. But before recruiting, teachers within the hiring district should be consulted in case they are interested in the position. To facilitate such moves, district teachers should be polled every several years about possible assignment changes. (See Figure 1.5 for a sample polling questionnaire.)

If no district teachers are interested in or qualified for the open position, the next task is to build the largest pool of applicants possible. Figure 1.6 provides 13 strategies for expanding the candidate pool.

Consulting Current Teachers

Current district teachers should be asked their advice on where to find good candidates. Because these teachers have already been through the district hiring process, they can offer great insight regarding its strengths and weaknesses; in addition, they know many of the key people to contact for advice, particularly teacher-education personnel, and can testify to the desirability of signing with the current district. The district should try to solicit teacher recruitment support from current faculty on an annual basis; not only is it helpful, but it sends the message that the district cares about the opinions of its staff.

1.4
Sample Job Description

Note: *The statements below describe the general nature and level of work expected from classroom teachers. They are not an exhaustive list of all responsibilities, duties, and skills required.*

Position Title
Classroom teachers (all grade levels)

General Description
Primary responsibilities include:
- ☞ Creating an opportunity to learn for all students
- ☞ Developing student cognitive capacity, intellectual skills, and respect for learning
- ☞ Fostering student self-esteem, motivation, and sense of civic responsibility

Prerequisites for employment:
Successful applicants will meet all qualifications and behavioral standards as set by the state. In accordance with certification requirements and the performance expectations of the district, all classroom teachers must meet the following employment criteria:
- ☞ Master's degree from an accredited college or university
- ☞ State teaching license
- ☞ Professional employment file that meets district standards
- ☞ Professional verification of successful classroom performance or student-teaching experience
- ☞ Evidence of willingness and ability to comply with performance standards as established by the Teacher Standards and Practices Commission
- ☞ Proof of sensitivity and respect for the diverse district population

Summary of Essential Functions
Teachers must:
- ☞ Meet attendance requirements
- ☞ Plan for and guide the learning process to help students achieve program, teacher, and student objectives
- ☞ Maintain a classroom atmosphere conducive to learning
- ☞ Implement useful diagnostic and assessment measures
- ☞ Select and use effective instructional methods and learning materials
- ☞ Establish a cooperative relationship with all assigned students
- ☞ Maintain open communication with parents
- ☞ Engage in ongoing professional-development activities
- ☞ Work collaboratively to achieve school goals

Beginning Salaries
Dependent on prior experience and license status

1.5
Sample Polling Questionnaire

Optional Survey of Current Teacher Assignment Preferences

Once in a while, teachers have the opportunity to be reassigned to other positions within the district. These moves most often are due to retirements, the creation of new positions, or changes in district needs. Your responses to the following questions will help us to better mach positions with personnel.

Name _____

Current assignment _____

Please describe your ideal assignment within the district. It could be in a different grade level, subject area, or even school.

Please describe possible assignments that would provide you with professional stimulation and variety. How much time do you think you would need to prepare for such an assignment? On what other resources might you need to rely?

Recruiting from Neighboring Districts

Members of either the Task Force or the Selection Committee should call or visit outstanding first- and second-year teachers in neighboring districts and inform them of job openings. Teachers

---

1.6
Strategies for Expanding the Hiring Pool

- ☛ Produce brochures, CDs, and videos about highlighting your district's results, resources, location, professional growth
- ☛ Foster relationships with education professors at universities and colleges
- ☛ Establish formal connections with teacher-education institutions
- ☛ Mail vacancy announcements to universities and colleges within 200 miles of the district
- ☛ Apprise the best first- and second-year teachers in neighboring districts of job openings
- ☛ Send your best selected people, including teachers of color, to nearby job fairs
- ☛ Routinely solicit hiring recommendations from current faculty and parents
- ☛ Find out where your current teachers came from
- ☛ Institute a district visitors program for prospective applicants
- ☛ Notify professional state student education associations of job vacancies
- ☛ Advertise in newspapers
- ☛ Start a Web site
- ☛ Register with online candidate listings on college and university Web sites

---

should be offered incentives that would motivate them to switch districts, such as increased pay or greater opportunities for professional development.

Learning From Other Districts

Members of the Task Force should check in with other districts to review their ideas on teacher hiring, and conduct cost-benefit analyses of their selection systems. If hirers are concerned about divulging competitive information, they might wish to ally with districts outside the state.

Attracting Candidates

All teachers want to

- ☞ Express themselves freely
- ☞ Develop a sense of achievement
- ☞ Have their work recognized
- ☞ Feel autonomous
- ☞ Have their teaching visions respected
- ☞ Be proud of their schools and districts
- ☞ Make a difference to their schools and districts
- ☞ Close economic and racial achievement gaps
- ☞ Work with parents to help their students
- ☞ Create a student-centered school administration
- ☞ Support hands-on, project-oriented lessons
- ☞ Be central to decisions about teaching, and not on the periphery
- ☞ Trust their coworkers
- ☞ Work for a district that delivers on its promises
- ☞ Lead balanced lives
- ☞ Develop their own curriculum

A combination of focus groups, surveys, and interviews with newly hired teachers is an excellent way to ascertain the criteria of successful candidates. Here are a few questions for the Task Force to ask:

- ☞ What attracts you to school districts?
- ☞ What did you already know about our district when you applied?
- ☞ Do you get the sense that our teachers like our district?
- ☞ Which of these is more important to you, and why:
  - ☞ salary vs. induction
  - ☞ grade or subject assignment vs. technology
  - ☞ community support vs. teacher collaboration

☞ geography vs. salary
☞ What are some pluses and minuses of our district, in your opinion?
☞ What specific concerns do you have as a beginning teacher?

Distinguishing the District

Hirers should specify the qualities that set their district apart by highlighting outstanding student achievements, museums, research centers, and business connections, as well as the benefits of the hiring school's location. Testimonials of ways in which new teachers have grown professionally in the district are also helpful.

Incentives and Disincentives

Recruitment should highlight incentives for candidates and mitigate disincentives. Competitive incentives could include, for example, policies under which new teachers receive their first paycheck before school begins. Disincentives include discourteous contacts, no information for applicants, and waiting without updates.

Campus Visits and Job Fairs

Visits to university campuses and regional job fairs are great recruitment strategies. Campus visits should be coordinated with university placement offices, which usually will provide informational tables for screening interviews and literature distribution. These types of visits provide selectors with good face-to-face contact with prospective applicants and help familiarize them with the kinds of questions that candidates ask. Members of the Task Force should create a standard 30-second sales pitch for recruiters to use at career fairs and during interviews.

Relationships with Colleges and Universities

Foster relationships with teacher-training institutions within 200 miles of your district. Familiarize yourself with the people, programs, and routines of the institutions. Teacher educators at these places have seen their students in action; district selectors should meet these educators in person and ask them about their most promising students.

Districts might also offer guest speakers for education classes or send instructional materials—such as study materials, student work samples, and tests—for use in college courses. University professors and student-teacher supervisors, along with public school teachers and administrators, should be available for interview teams formed for preservice program admissions.

Brochures, Fliers, Videos, and CD-ROMs

Members of the Task Force should create colorful brochures that highlight the hiring district. These can be easily distributed and should include contact information and a list of steps to take when applying. Hirers should begin with black and white prototypes of fly-ers and gradually refine them; visit local printers and quick-copy out-lets for advice on design techniques. To save costs, volunteer parent teams can be enlisted to help with the production and folding of fly-ers. Aggressive, candidate-based marketing fliers, such as the example in Figure 1.7, should be considered. Videos, too, can sell the energy and personality of a district, particularly if skillfully produced by specialists. If video reproduction costs are prohibitive, CD-ROMs provide an inexpensive yet content-heavy alternative; unlike videos, CDs are cheap enough to give away.

Newspaper Advertisements

Newspaper advertisements can inform candidates all over the coun-try about district openings. Many job ads today are online; *Education*

1.7
Sample Recruitment Flyer

Note: *The King City School District is fictional; Web sites and contact information are provided as examples only.*

The King City School District

Why teach with us?
Because our teachers:

- **Lead.** At the King City School District, teachers write, select, and sequence their own curriculum and instruction
- **Collaborate.** We schedule regular times and places where teachers can plan their work together
- **Inspire.** Our district is organized around teacher work and performance

- **Develop.** We provide beginners with mentors, support groups, consultants, and special training
- **Create.** King City teachers help formulate the district's teaching strategies and assessment procedures
- **Stay.** Our teachers remain in the district an average of 22 years

For more information, visit us on the Web at: www.teacher-royalty.org or www.kingcity.k12.va.us
For more information, contact:
Betty Johnson • 555-123-4567 (phone) • 555-234-5678 (fax) • betty@kingcity.k.12.va.us (e-mail)

Week, for instance, posts teacher openings on its Web site regularly. (The site can be accessed at http://www.edweek.org/jobs.cfm; see Appendix A for more online hiring resources.) Items to include in advertisements are

- ☞ Licensing requirements
- ☞ Beginning date of employment
- ☞ List of required and optional forms, transcripts, and recommendations
- ☞ Application deadline
- ☞ List of hiring policies (e.g., affirmative action)
- ☞ Contact information

District Web Sites

A district Web site is a perfect place to announce job openings and provide general district information. (A good example is the New Haven Unified School District site, at http://www.nhusd.k12.ca.us/.) Particularly large districts may have one Web site dedicated to staff along with another, more comprehensive site devoted to ongoing district business. Staff sites can offer descriptions of procedures, online forms, application deadlines, photos of the district, purpose statements, and links to local resources (e.g., real estate agencies, symphonies, and newspapers).

Visitors Programs

A visitors program is an excellent way to show off a district or school. The Task Force might consider scheduling tours of the district for interested candidates, including classroom visits and meetings with recent hires.

Recruiting Diverse Teachers

School faculties should reflect the diversity of their districts. Successful recruitment will address the wishes of all teachers: physical safety, good curriculum, effective bureaucracy, high parental involvement, good fellow teachers, and adequate funding. Because past injustices have historically made it difficult for minorities to demonstrate their true potential, minority recruitment is morally just; at the same time, mere membership in a protected class rarely is cause enough to offer priority in hiring.

Teacher selectors should be aware of their own social status when making decisions. For example, my status as an older white male at times makes me less sensitive to the comparatively restricted mobility, greater social pressure to conform, and stricter behavioral expectations that exist for women, minorities, and young people in society. Equal opportunities for all do not yet exist, and racism continues to plague society.

A good mix of women and men of different ethnic and economic backgrounds, combined with diversity-driven recruitment, education, monitoring, discussion, and analysis, is a good way to remedy social inequality. The best hiring practices do away with unfair barriers and make extraordinary efforts to include all talented and hard working candidates in the candidate pool.

The Selection Committee should ask itself the following questions:

- ☞ How well represented are minorities among district teachers, relative to the community?
- ☞ How well do the district's minority teachers understand our strategies for (and barriers to) ensuring a diverse pool of applicants?
- ☞ Do we address this issue as a legal, social, and moral one? How should we deal with the concerns of minority teachers?
- ☞ How well are current recruitment techniques working?

☞ Are there any issues that currently deter minority candidates from applying to the district?

☞ How does the district support its minority teachers?

☞ Are there minorities at all district levels, including administration and leadership?

☞ How do the district's minority teachers rate its outreach strategies?

The district should also consider the following strategies for minority recruitment:

☞ Use the Internet and teacher listing services

☞ Involve minority recruiters

☞ Schedule mock interviews with candidates in order to provide them with information about the school and encourage them to apply

☞ Establish "Meet and Greet" nights managed by minority staff

☞ Follow the progress of word-of-mouth information by noting who's talking to whom

☞ Advertise in publications with large minority readerships

☞ Recruit at colleges and universities with particularly diverse populations

☞ Enlist the help of local professional organizations with minority recruitment

☞ Mention the importance of diversity to the district in all recruitment materials

☞ Send job announcements and district materials to religious centers (temples, mosques, churches), political action groups (NAACP chapters), and clubs

☞ Form alliances with teacher education programs at colleges and universities; exchange speakers and sample curriculum materials

- ☞ Support Future Teachers of America clubs in the district's middle schools and high schools, and recruit minority students to join
- ☞ Link with community colleges and universities for long-term development of minority candidates
- ☞ Work with local universities to train the district's minority aides, paraeducators, and clerical staff
- ☞ Ask minority teachers about relatives, family, or friends who might be interested in working for the district
- ☞ Solicit minority student teachers; offer stipends, books, transportation, and teaching supplies
- ☞ Establish cash signing bonuses for all new hires
- ☞ Make contracts available early in the hiring season
- ☞ Contribute to or raise funds for college and university minority scholarships
- ☞ Arrange with community businesses and service organizations to reduce moving, rental, and banking costs
- ☞ Create summer employment opportunities
- ☞ Support local minority-teacher networks
- ☞ Assign and monitor minority mentors
- ☞ Design staged entry assignments—i.e., simple at first, then more and more challenging
- ☞ Arrange specialized advanced degree programs with local universities
- ☞ Offer technology grants to minorities: PCs for home, laptop computers, teacher management software, regular consultant time and assistance, Internet service
- ☞ Train faculty on how to support and retain minority colleagues

The NEA maintains a helpful Web site on many of these topics at http://www.nea.org/recruit/minority/.

Part-time Teaching and Job Sharing

District support of part-time teaching and job sharing is controversial but makes sense: it enlarges the applicant pool, resulting in better hires; favors energetic teachers who can multitask well; and helps discourage teacher absenteeism. School districts that accept part-time teachers stand to hire talent that is simply unavailable to less flexible districts.

Special Provisions for Outstanding Candidates

Losing a desirable candidate to another district is an obvious risk of the hiring process. To counteract this danger, districts might want to create a fast-track system for top contenders, including accelerated meeting schedules and quick reference checks.

Abbreviated Hiring

If a teacher resigns at the very beginning of the school year, or if there are very few applicants for a position, an abbreviated hiring system is advisable. Under these circumstances, one small group of selectors should be charged with all the necessary duties, and reference phone calls should be reduced to one or two per candidate.

Findings of Academic Research

Harris and Eder (1999) have concluded that
- The use of multiple selectors benefits the hiring process
- Hiring decisions should be based on candidate accomplishments rather than attitude or potential
- Structured interviews usually are more reliable than spontaneous ones

☛ Hirers should pay particular attention to general verbal ability in addition to experience

Action Validation

Technically precise teacher-selection validity is difficult to discern at present because precise validation measures don't exist. By applying to itself the criteria for effective hiring outlined in this chapter—and by proving its adherence to them—the Selection Committee can and should demonstrate its own validity.

Once a selection committee has been created, candidates have been recruited, and detailed hiring procedures have been established, it is time to start narrowing the pool of applicants.

2

FIRST-LEVEL SCREENING

When the pool of candidates is at its largest, the district Screening
Team should require all applicants to submit data corroborating their
track records; this is the first of three screening levels, each of which
requires applicants to submit different materials (see Figure 2.1).

At the first stage of screening, past performance results should
take precedence over candidate disposition or presumed potential. For
beginning teachers in particular, track records are bound to be somewhat ambiguous. Beginners will usually have spent a limited amount
of time student teaching, and under strictly controlled circumstances
at that.

It is difficult to determine whether a candidate is qualified to teach
based solely on the paper evidence; after all, a well-written resume
does not necessarily imply classroom expertise. The Screening Team,
therefore, should ask candidates for a variety of materials on which to
base its decisions. Even then, no candidate is likely to supply all of the
data requested, and the Screening Team will need to make its recommendations based on assorted combinations of evidence.

Although an entirely objective judgment is nearly impossible to
achieve based on application data alone, past performance patterns are
often accurate predictors of future achievement. In all cases, election

---

2.1
Evidence for Different Levels of Screening

At each level of screening, hirers should evaluate the following criteria:

First-Level Screening (all applicants)	Second-Level Screening (top four to seven applicants)	Third-Level Screening (top three applicants)
☞ Application forms	☞ Work samples or portfolios	☞ Additional follow-up calls
☞ Resumes	☞ Videotapes	☞ Additional interviews
☞ Cover letters	☞ Follow-up phone calls	☞ Performance sample
☞ Recommendations	☞ Extended resume	☞ Personal visits to references
☞ Job experience	☞ Essays	☞ Group interviews
☞ Written statements	☞ District-made tests	☞ Additional essay
☞ Professional-knowledge tests	☞ Interviews	

---

is a matter of deciding relative value rather than establishing absolute merit. The collective expert and subjective judgment of the Screening Team, if properly staffed, will no doubt prove thoroughly reliable as long as the team is provided with the following information:

- ☞ Application form
- ☞ Resume
- ☞ Cover letter
- ☞ Postsecondary course transcripts
- ☞ Recommendations
- ☞ Test scores

In addition to application forms, some districts provide candidates with legal release forms, allowing districts access to confidential information (see Figure 2.2).

2.2
Sample Applicant Release Form

Note: *This sample is only a model. Districts should employ the services of legal counsel when crafting release forms of their own.*

I understand that, pursuant to my application for a teaching position, the King City School District may request information relevant to my application from educational institutions, personal and professional references, past employers, and professional licensing agencies. The district reserves the right to contact references outside of those provided in my application.

I understand that review of my application may include a review of any criminal records.

I hereby consent to the release of information relevant to my application for employment. Such information may include, but not be limited to, dates of employment or education and work and academic performance assessments. I authorize former supervisors, instructors, or employers to respond to verbal or written inquiries from the King City School District.

I understand that all information received or created by the district as a result of my application for employment will be treated as confidential information; will not be released to me except as required by law; and will be destroyed after having served its initial purpose (as determined by the district).

Name: _____ Date: _____

I do not authorize the King City School District to
___ Contact educational institutions, personal and professional references, past employers, and professional licensing agencies.
___ Contact references other than those provided to the district in my application.

Name: _____ Date: _____

Application Form

In order to create a truly effective application form, the district should study application forms from other districts, double-check layout for readability and clarity of directions, and pilot test a preliminary version of the form. District application forms should check for critical requirements, such as degrees and recommendations from accredited institutions; unlike resumes, they can be crafted at the district's discretion to ask specific questions (Figure 2.3).

Application forms should include room for the candidate to provide supplemental information, although the Screening Team can safely ignore any general background data (e.g., characteristics of one's hometown, high school extracurricular activities) and a statement authorizing the district to contact references in order to verify information.

The district should be careful to ensure that the forms do not solicit any irrelevant information that might bias the hirers, (e.g., family status or a photo of the applicant). If, however, the district wishes to ascertain potentially discriminatory information purely for demographic purposes, the form could include a detachable postcard for the candidate to fill in and return anonymously.

All forms should be available in hard copy, in electronic format for transmission via e-mail, and in a downloadable format on district Web sites. Some states offer common online application forms for use by individual districts (go to http://www.ospa.k12.or.us/otsstart.htm for an example). Completed electronic forms should be kept in computer databases for future reference.

Resume

Unlike application forms, resumes allow candidates the leeway to express themselves as they see fit and don't cost the district a cent to produce. By reviewing every resume carefully, interviewers can develop

2.3
Sample District Application Form

Name:

Social Security Number:

Address:

Phone: Fax:
E-Mail:

Position(s) sought (grade level and subject):

Choose one: Full time ___   Part time ___   Substitute ___

Please list any other subjects you are licensed to teach:

Please list any activities you are qualified to direct or coach:

Date you are available to work:

Dates you are available for interview:

Licenses held:

Endorsements:

(continued on next page)

Reference contact information:

Schools and dates attended:

Education work experience:

Other work experience:

Tests taken and scores received (e.g., Praxis, GRE):

Languages spoken, written, or read, other than English:

Honors and special training:

Relatives employed by the district:

How did you find out about the district? About the position?

If currently under contract, can you be released if we offer you a position?

Has your license ever been suspended or revoked?

Have you ever been dismissed or asked to resign?

(continued on next page)

Have you ever plead guilty to or been convicted of a felony or misdemeanor?

Discrimination in hiring due to age, sex, race, color, religion, marital status, national origin, ancestry, physical or mental handicap unrelated to job performance, military status, or sexual orientation is unfair and interferes with good teacher hiring. Please exclude any information that indicates membership in any of the categories above.

Please sign below to (a) indicate that all the information above is true, and (b) authorize the district to contact all necessary sources for verification.
Name: _____ Date: _____

Additional Directions for Applying to Our District
In addition to this application form, please provide us with the following:
  ☞ Resume
  ☞ Placement file (or letters of recommendation and postsecondary transcripts, if placement file not available)
  ☞ Test scores from all available educational tests

If you are selected at our first level of screening, you will be asked to immediately send the following:
  ☞ Extended resume (two to three pages long)
  ☞ Brief essay on a topic furnished by the district
  ☞ Copy of portfolio or work sample, if available (will not be returned)
  ☞ URLs of Web sites you have created
  ☞ Other information you think would be helpful

In addition, you will be asked to complete both a district multiple-choice test and one or more interviews.

If you are selected as a finalist for the position, you will be asked to immediately provide us with the following:
  ☞ Brief essay on a second topic furnished by the district
  ☞ A videotape of your teaching
  ☞ Other information you think would be helpful

In addition, you will be asked to complete one or more interviews and a 30-minute teaching episode with students.

personalized questions for each candidate. Because resumes can be formatted electronically, they can also easily be stored in a computer database.

There are two major types of resumes: chronological and experiential. In chronological resumes, education and work experiences are listed sequentially in the order in which they happened; experiential resumes are organized according to competencies, accomplishments, and credentials. A combined format presents important information, such as employers, credentials, and specific educational institutions, but also a sense of direction and accomplishment.

An experienced reviewer can read a resume and assess its worth in about 45 seconds. To compare different styles and get a feel for the variety of candidates, individuals or teams of three to five should review resumes in batches during uninterrupted sessions. In the case of group reviews, individual comments should be consolidated on group report forms. Team reviews add vitality to the hiring process by allowing reviewers to watch and learn from each other.

Dailey (1982) calls the resume a show of "the privileges a person has had—the opportunities awarded—not the performance in those positions" and maintains that a resume is "incomplete until the interviewer has 'cross examined' the candidate about what it means" (p. 87). Reviewers should be sure not to dwell overmuch on impressive but irrelevant details, such as Peace Corps service or hobbies. See Figure 2.4 for a list of what to look for in a resume.

The resume review should involve two steps: an initial screening, followed by a second quality check. During the initial screening, reviewers should look for the following characteristics:

- ☛ Formatting doesn't distract from the information presented
- ☛ Sequence of events and items listed is clear and logical
- ☛ Education listed includes specific dates, institutions, and degrees

2.4
Checklist for Resume Review

☛ Information is well organized, easy to read and understand
☛ Specific successes and accomplishments are highlighted
☛ Evidence of versatility and variety of experience
☛ Evidence of initiative and team membership
☛ Enumeration of specific credentials, such as licenses, diplomas, and certificates
☛ Goals and priorities are clearly defined and match the applicant's experience and training
☛ Experience listed is pertinent to open position
☛ Previously held positions indicate scope of applicant's responsibility
☛ Skills, talents, and education are confirmed by track record
☛ Evidence of continuous, self-initiated professional development
☛ Solid writing skills
☛ Attention to detail, no mistakes
☛ No unaccounted-for gaps in time line of educational and professional experience

☛ List of teaching credentials or licenses includes specific names, levels, and locations

☛ Experience listed indicates potential strengths and past successes

☛ Affiliations and activities listed are relevant to the position and reflect genuine accomplishments

☛ Every reference listed includes a description of the person's relationship to applicant and contact information

☛ Applicant's contact information appears, including mailing address, phone, and e-mail

At this early stage, it is especially important to consider discriminatory information carefully. Any mention of race, age, religious affiliations, or political activity should be blacked out on resumes before the second review stage, except in cases where the information sheds light on the work-related skills (e.g., a leadership role in a support group, or at church). Reviewers should always keep from drawing conclusions about applicants, whether positive or negative, based on discriminatory information. Juan Gomez, for instance, may neither want nor be able to speak Spanish, just as an Egyptian national may have no interest in Middle Eastern issues.

During this quality check, reviewers should keep in mind the following:

- ☛ **Job relevancy.** How pertinent is the applicant's previous experience to the open position? How recent is the experience?
- ☛ **Job match.** Visualize the applicant in the open position. If the position is in a 2nd-grade classroom, does the candidate have experience with younger children? If it's a high school drama program, does the applicant appear interested in theater?
- ☛ **Assumptions.** Be wary of hidden truths: four years at college does not indicate completion of a degree; cochair of a committee may refer to a council of two.
- ☛ **Red flags.** Be on alert for vagueness, qualifications ("familiar" or "acquainted with"), "padding" of experience with trivial information.
- ☛ **Be reasonable and flexible.** Resumes are inherently restrictive; look for outstanding details.

Cover Letter

Cover letters can provide clues to an applicant's capability. Reviewers should watch for

- ☛ Proper spelling and grammar

☛ Correct formatting
☛ Statements specific to the hiring district or position, indicating extra effort
☛ Candidate's overall professionalism and drive

Postsecondary Course Transcripts

Transcripts from college or university courses can be useful windows into each candidate's area of expertise. Naturally, applicants are especially well prepared to teach subjects they have studied at advanced levels. Transcripts can also offer a glimpse at the candidate's learning curve, and at his or her progress over time.

Grades are by no means foolproof indicators of teaching skills; applicants with poor grades might plausibly suggest that they can better understand the plight of lower achieving students. But districts should be careful not to discount grades altogether: many authors have reported an anti-intellectual bias in public school teacher hiring (Perry, 1981; Wise, Darling-Hammond, & Berry, 1987a).

Teacher-Education Training

The Screening Team should always take into account the applicant's teacher-education training. Typically, universities will offer four-year undergraduate programs or fifth-year programs. Each has different strengths: undergraduate programs teach principles of education over the course of a student's school career, while fifth-year programs concentrate on liberal arts for the first four years and on pedagogical instruction in the fifth. Either kind of program can turn out excellent teachers.

According to the National Center for Education Statistics (1997), more than half of all U.S. teachers come from unaccredited teacher-education institutions. Accredited schools have a variety of advantages, such as credentialed faculty and proven evaluation systems. The National Council for Accreditation of Teacher Education (NCATE) sets and monitors important standards regarding faculty training, school funding, and use of evaluation data for program improvement. Other national organizations—such as the American Association of Colleges for Teacher Education (AACTE), the Holmes Group, and the Interstate New Teacher Assessment and Support Consortium (INTASC)—can provide the Screening Team with valuable information regarding the relative quality of teacher education programs. (See Appendix B for the Web sites of these and other useful resources.)

The Screening Team should assign one or two members to research teacher-preparation institutions and keep the information in its files for future reference.

Recommendations

The Screening Team should be sure to get five to six references from the finalists. Recommendations are especially helpful when they include comparisons with other education students and specific highlights or vignettes of the applicant at work. Written recommendations are necessary in the hiring process, but they do have some drawbacks. Too often, recommendations

- ☞ Ignore the applicant's negative characteristics
- ☞ Are unrepresentative of general performance
- ☞ Favor descriptions of general traits over behavioral examples
- ☞ Are provided by personal friends, whose opinions too often are subjective
- ☞ Present character testimony alone

The most helpful recommendations are from those who have seen the candidate working with students; a cooperating teacher from the applicant's student-teaching days would be ideal. University student-teaching supervisors are also good sources, as they generally interact with large numbers of education students, whose qualities they are especially fit to discern. In most hiring situations, both sources will be in agreement about the candidate's ability. Building administrators from the applicant's previous teaching or student-teaching job can also be informative references, but they are usually less familiar with student-teacher performance than are cooperating teachers and supervisors. A single tepid recommendation should never preclude a candidate from further consideration.

Additional recommendations may be helpful, but a large number of testimonials may be more reflective of candidate networking skills than classroom performance. An especially driven applicant may spend a lot of time grooming potential references, while a superior candidate may not have had the same opportunity.

Letters of recommendation that are especially important, such as those mentioned above, need to be considered if at all possible; if the candidate has not provided them, the Screening Team should obtain them on its own. There is no persuasive empirical evidence regarding closed or open files, although some people think that keeping information from the candidate encourages greater frankness.

Educational recommendations are distinct from references in the business world because the experiences they describe are so unlike the open position. During teacher hiring, the applicant's former position will often have had little to do with education, and student teaching is completely different from the autonomous routine of classroom teaching.

Educational recommendations tend to be more positive than those found in the business world. In business, employees switch jobs either because they are fired, laid off, or unhappy at work; when teachers seek employment, on the other hand, they are moving from one positive setting (college, business employment) to another positive setting (the classroom).

The Screening Team should carefully analyze negative comments from references, which may not necessarily reflect the applicant's worth. For example, a current employer may be angry at the candidate's decision to leave and consequently malign the applicant out of spite. Half (1985) recommends that hirers give the candidate a chance to explain any negative appraisals without revealing the source, and to "ask for names of people who might verify the candidate's version" (p. 156).

Some people think recommendations should be completely frank, and that they are most credible when they reveal certain minor reservations about the candidate. Others maintain that the purpose of recommendations is to *recommend*—that the sole responsibility of a reference is to help the candidate land a job. Many references are reluctant to criticize applicants for fear of being charged with slander, libel, or defamation of character (although in recent years, a number of states have enacted "good faith" reference protection).

When checking references, hirers should keep a list of legally precluded topics—such as marital status or religious practices—on hand. They should also remember to ask the applicant's permission before contacting a reference.

Teacher Test Scores

Tests can speak volumes about candidates by reflecting their problem-solving skills and level of professional knowledge. Testing is now a much greater part of state licensing than in the past, so most applicants should have scores available for review. Assessment centers, in which professionals are put through a battery of written and performance measures, exist for veteran teachers but not for beginners.

In 1997, the National Center for Education Statistics reported that 49 percent of U.S. school districts required teacher applicants to pass a state test of basic educational skills, 39 percent tested applicants on subject matter, and 39 percent used the National Teachers Examination (NTE). (The Center found that state tests are more frequently used in the South and Midwest, while the NTE prevails in the Northeast.)

Michael Scriven (1990) is one of the few experts to recommend that hirers seriously consider the applicant's subject-matter knowledge in the selection process. Tests are particularly well suited to this purpose because reviewers don't need to be versed in the subject matter themselves: exams are statistically reliable indicators of expertise. But assessment based on test results has its downside. Tests represent knowledge acquired, which is not the same as actual performance. The ability to do well on a test does not automatically connote good teaching skills. And despite the apparent validity of subject-matter tests, they are not greatly respected by teachers as hiring tools (Peterson, 2000). It is odd that a profession so heavily reliant on exams should take issue with hiring tests, but teachers do have their reasons—among them:

- ☞ Tests are not fair to all who take them
- ☞ Some excellent teachers test poorly
- ☞ Other factors, such as classroom management skills, are better indicators of teaching potential
- ☞ A direct connection between tests and teacher performance has not yet been established
- ☞ Only minimal subject-matter knowledge is necessary for classroom teaching

Tests of attitude, personality, motivation, and honesty are seldom if ever valid assessment tools, and most are illegal for job hiring purposes. Not only do the questions asked on such tests run the risk of invading the test taker's privacy, but the U.S. Supreme Court ruled in *Griggs v. Duke Power Company* (1971) that a direct connection must exist between tests and job performance in order for them to be used in hiring. The EEOC permits hirers to use tests, but only if they do not unfairly discriminate among ethnic groups.

Selectors should always keep test data confidential. It is interesting that most hirers perceive interviews as fairer gauges of potential performance than tests, because they permit the applicants to speak for themselves.

✓   ✓   ✓

SECOND- AND THIRD-LEVEL SCREENING

In order to reduce the pool of candidates to three, the Screening Team should ask each remaining applicant to provide an extended resume, a short essay, a portfolio and work samples, and addresses of any relevant personal or professional Web sites. The Screening Team should also place additional calls to references, conduct thorough background checks, and interview each applicant twice. (Candidates should be advised of every step in the hiring process upon initially submitting their application forms.) The Screening Team should neither expect nor require candidates to supply all the information asked for at this stage; selections should simply be based on the best information available.

Extended Resumes

The Screening Team should ask the current pool of applicants to submit via fax, mail, or e-mail extended resumes of two to three pages in length, including explanations, contextual information, and detailed examples of achievement. These should be analyzed according to the same procedures discussed in Chapter 2.

Candidate Essays

The Screening Team should present the candidates with two essay questions that address their teaching philosophies and problem-solving skills. For example:

- ☞ What would you do if your students begin to segregate themselves according to their cultural or ethnic backgrounds? Write for 20 minutes about your strategies for helping diverse students to interact. How would you teach them to work and play together regardless of their differences?
- ☞ State one important concept from your subject area. Tell us in 20 minutes how you would teach this concept to students for maximum comprehension.
- ☞ What would you do if some of your students consistently finish their work ahead of others?

Responses should be one to three pages long, and applicants should be assured that there are no definite right or wrong answers. The Screening Team should take note of applicants who communicate their ideas clearly, justify their strategies, and consider alternate points of view.

Essays, of course, represent abstract goals and strategies rather than concrete classroom experience. They tend to favor applicants who write smoothly and are well versed in current education issues, and should be especially beneficial to applicants who feel nervous with face-to-face interviews. The Screening Team can either allow reviewers to judge the essays at their own discretion or construct a standard scoring guide for the purpose. At the very least, the reviewers should be apprised of characteristics to look out for. Reviewers should not automatically discount applicants whose views aren't 100 percent in line with those of the district; diversity of opinion, after all, helps to strengthen schools. The first round of essays can be written offsite, but finalists will have to write the second on location.

Portfolios

Campbell and colleagues (1997) define a teacher's portfolio as:

> . . . not merely a file of course projects and assignments, nor . . . a scrapbook of teaching memorabilia. A portfolio is an organized, goal-driven documentation of your professional growth and achieved competence in the complex act called teaching. Although it is a collection of documents, a portfolio is tangible evidence of . . . knowledge, dispositions, and skills that you possess as a growing professional. . . . [Portfolio documents] are self-selected, reflecting your individuality and autonomy (p. 3).

Among the items that applicants might include in their portfolios are those listed in Figure 3.1.

Portfolios may be organized according to specific guidelines—such as those available from the National Association for the Education of Young Children (NAEYC) or the National Art Education Association (NAEA)—or as reflective of a set of teacher criteria, such as those devised by the Interstate New Teacher Assessment and Support Consortium (INTASC, 1992; Figure 3.2).

A short portfolio may be limited to ten pages, while a longer one might require a storage box or outsize container. Both should include lesson and management plans, letters of recommendation, and samples of student work. Portfolios should consist of photocopies not original material, and should be destroyed by the district at a predetermined stage (e.g., six months after filling the position).

Work Samples

Work samples should include traditional unit plans developed by the applicant, along with goal analyses, discussions of context (e.g., class size, student characteristics), instructional materials, pre- and post-instruction evaluations, and student learning self-assessments. Taken as a whole, work samples can indicate each candidate's

3.1
Possible Portfolio Items

- ☞ Anecdotal records
- ☞ Case studies of individual student learning or behavior
- ☞ Student assessments
- ☞ Videos of students or the candidate at work
- ☞ Floor plans showing classroom arrangements
- ☞ Classroom management plans
- ☞ Classroom bulletin-board items
- ☞ Curriculum plans
- ☞ Cooperative-learning ideas
- ☞ Essays
- ☞ Field-trip plans
- ☞ Parent and student comments about the applicant
- ☞ Evaluations
- ☞ Goal statements
- ☞ Letters to parents
- ☞ Journal entries
- ☞ Lesson plans
- ☞ Individualized learning plans for mainstreamed students
- ☞ Peer critiques
- ☞ A list of computer programs used by the applicant in class
- ☞ Meeting and workshop logs
- ☞ Miscellaneous observations
- ☞ Photos of students, field trips, classroom arrangements, etc.
- ☞ Article summaries and critiques that describe key but unusual features of the candidate's teaching program
- ☞ Evidence of media competencies
- ☞ Projects
- ☞ Philosophy statement
- ☞ Student portfolios and work samples
- ☞ References
- ☞ Problem-solving logs
- ☞ Professional development plan
- ☞ Student reading list
- ☞ Student contracts
- ☞ Classroom materials created by the applicant
- ☞ Classroom magazine subscriptions
- ☞ Seating arrangement diagrams
- ☞ Rule and procedures charts
- ☞ Schedules
- ☞ Self-assessments
- ☞ Descriptions of work experience
- ☞ Transcripts
- ☞ Theme studies
- ☞ Descriptions of volunteering experience
- ☞ Unit plans
- ☞ Awards and certificates

3.2
Topical Standards of Teacher Competency as Developed by the Interstate New Teacher Assessment and Support Consortium (INTASC)

Applicants should consider including materials in their portfolios that reflect the following competencies:

☞ **Knowledge of Subject Matter.** Concepts, tools of inquiry, structure
☞ **Knowledge of Human Development and Learning.** Intellectual, social, personal
☞ **Adapting Instruction for Individual Needs.** Diverse learners
☞ **Multiple Instructional Strategies.** Critical thinking, problem solving, performance, direct instruction
☞ **Classroom Motivation and Management.** Individual and group
☞ **Communication Skills.** Verbal, nonverbal, media
☞ **Instructional Planning.** Subject matter, students, community
☞ **Assessment of Student Learning.** Formal, informal, physical, social, mental
☞ **Professional Commitment and Responsibility.** Reflective practice, organizations
☞ **Partnerships.** Colleagues, parents, community

Source: Interstate New Teacher Assessment and Support Consortium (1992). *Model standards for beginning teacher licensing and development.* Washington, DC: Council of Chief State School Officers.

☞ Resourcefulness
☞ Degree of allegiance to district, state, and national frameworks
☞ Ability to align goals, curriculum, and assessment
☞ Assessment capabilities
☞ Attention to student achievement

Telephone Follow-ups

The Screening Team should place follow-up telephone calls to verify or supplement information gleaned from resumes, recommendations, and interviews for the four to six remaining applicants. Candidates should have their references consent to follow-up calls prior to submitting their names to the Screening Team. The Screening Team should contact people who have actually seen the candidate teach, such as principals, university or practicum supervisors, or cooperating teachers from student-teaching programs. When making follow-up calls, hirers should

- ☛ Conduct job-related conversations rather than asking about appearance, personality, or style
- ☛ Keep a list handy of questions to avoid
- ☛ Pay special attention to those who have most recently worked with the applicant
- ☛ Be friendly and positive; develop a rapport
- ☛ Use a script
- ☛ Take notes
- ☛ Restate questions and answers for confirmation
- ☛ Ask about possible additional references
- ☛ Pay attention to voice tone; note whether the candidate is positive and enthusiastic or curt and guarded
- ☛ Read between the lines
- ☛ Allow references to interpret and even misconstrue questions—let them help guide the discussion
- ☛ Offer to reciprocate and act as references themselves, should the need arise

In addition, hirers might want to use the form provided in Figure 3.3 to help structure and document follow-up calls.

During follow-up calls, hirers should focus on verifying objective information—i.e., locations, dates, duties, credentials—as well as job-

related characteristics. They should also be sure to use the term "verification" as well as "reference."

3.3
Follow-up Phone-Call Form

Candidate Name: _____

Desired Position: _____

Date of Call: _____

Name of Reference: _____

Role of Reference: _____

Circle all that apply:

     PRE-INTERVIEW   POST-INTERVIEW   SECOND CALL

Ask reference to confirm relevant dates, locations, duties and credentials
provided by applicant.

Questions

What do you think of the candidate as a teacher?

_____

_____

Can you provide any outstanding examples of the candidate's behavior?

_____

_____

What are the candidate's strong points?

_____

_____

(continued on next page)

What are the candidate's limitations?

_____

_____

How long have you been familiar with candidate's work?

_____

_____

How would you describe the candidate's work ethic?

_____

_____

What is the candidate's relationship with the school community like?

_____

_____

How does the candidate compare to other teachers/students/student teachers you have worked with?

_____

_____

Does the candidate foster student learning?

_____

_____

Would you hire this person yourself?

_____

_____

(continued on next page)

What did the candidate do, if anything, that was unexpected or out of the ordinary?

_____

_____

Are there any other references we could contact?

_____

_____

Is there anything you would like to add about the candidate?

_____

_____

Comment on the candidate's
- ☛ Subject matter knowledge
- ☛ Pedagogical knowledge
- ☛ Track record of student achievement
- ☛ Proficiency with instructional materials
- ☛ Classroom management skills

_____

_____

_____

_____

_____

_____

_____

_____

_____

_____

Some references may be unwilling to divulge much information for fear of being sued. To encourage frankness, callers should assure them that the follow-up is necessary to ensure a fair and objective decision, that the district has a right to ask these questions, and that all answers will be kept strictly confidential.

District-Made Tests

The National Center for Education Statistics estimated in 1997 that district-made standardized tests were used in hiring by approximately 3 percent of the nation's 15,000 school districts; Wise, Darling-Hammond, and Berry (1987a) found them commonly used only in districts that performed exceptionally well. The tests could include questions about school law, test design and usage, curriculum reform issues, developmental psychology, instructional methodology, and discipline strategies. All questions, of course, should be directly related to job performance. Directions and scoring rubric should be made clear from the outset, and should be the same for all applicants. Testing dates should be flexible, in case candidates fall ill or become otherwise indisposed.

Physical Screening

Limited physical screening of teacher candidates is permitted under law, to ensure that applicants are free of communicable diseases and to check their work endurance levels.

Additional Information

After carefully assessing the information provided by the four to six remaining candidates, the Screening Team should select three finalists, who should in turn provide the district with a videotape of the candidate teaching and a performance sample or microteaching session.

Videotape of Teaching

Videotapes of teacher candidates in the classroom are becoming increasingly common, and in fact are now necessary for National Board certification. While they can offer telling glimpses of the applicant's facility with students, it is impossible to ascertain from videos the full measure of an applicant's proficiency. The quality of videotapes depends largely on editing, camera position, and sound fidelity; several cameras are better than one alone, as they tend to provide greater scope.

Too often, videos communicate little about the appropriateness of teacher behavior. In addition, they

- ☞ Don't provide an opportunity to ask students what they think is going on
- ☞ Document classroom behavior rather than student learning
- ☞ Rarely show the teacher dealing with unexpected events or problems
- ☞ Often represent ideal times of the day and week
- ☞ Tend not to present enough context for classroom events
- ☞ Disrupt classrooms, subtly altering student and teacher behavior
- ☞ Rarely reflect typical performance

As a matter of fairness and accuracy, the Screening Team should view all tapes in their entirety.

Performance Sample or Microteaching

A performance sample is a 20- to 40-minute, candidate-led classroom lesson conducted at the hiring school. One to three members of the Screening Team should observe the lesson, along with the students' usual teacher (who should have the final say on the objective for the lesson).

Performance samples are good at showing extemporaneous teaching abilities and can serve as a tiebreaker for similarly qualified candidates. The Screening Team should focus on

☞ The applicant's confidence, energy, and patience

☞ Exceptional communication skills or problems

☞ Exceptional sensitivity, flexibility, and accommodation of students

The Screening Team should exercise caution when using performance samples to judge applicants. On-the-spot teaching is a singular practice, and many superb teachers can look awkward taking part. Scriven (1990) cautions against trial teaching, "because the teacher is going in cold, is not there for long enough for observers to pick up a sense of . . . conscientiousness and perseverance, and is under atypical stress" (p. 91).

Some candidates might be at a disadvantage because their strength lies in additive instruction over time. The presence of observers distorts the situation further, by altering student behavior. Unless several observers are present, minority points of view may sway judgments about the candidate. In addition, student achievement results for one-time lessons are unreliable. Hirers should keep the following issues in mind when analyzing microteaching lessons:

☞ Many important qualities, such as perseverance, are not observable

☞ Time restrictions mean limited student learning

☞ Teaching style might conflict with observers' preferences

☞ Limited number of observers

☞ Class sizes and behavior patterns vary greatly

☛ Teacher reaction is important, but 30 minutes is a small sample of a teacher's total repertoire

☛ Presence of other adults in the classroom might alter performance

☛ Difficult to separate talent from experience in a performance situation

☛ Competitive context is quite different from classroom teaching

Once the top three candidates have been selected, they should be ranked in order of preference and their names reported to the superintendent.

4

THE HIRING INTERVIEW

I have devoted this entire chapter to interviews because of their
extensive use, detailed complexity, specific limitations, and demanding logistics. Realizing the potential of interviews depends on skill,
preparation, and good timing.

According to Messmer (1998), a candidate's ability to create a
good impression during an interview doesn't necessarily translate into
effective teaching. As common as they are in teacher hiring, interviews frequently are used too early in the selection process and tend
to overemphasize personal qualities that have nothing to do with the
classroom. However, at later stages of hiring, interviews help clarify
data from other sources, provide additional information about the
applicant, and eliminate candidates who have trouble answering basic
questions.

Benefits of Interviews

Interviews make sense. What could be better than asking candidates
questions face to face—watching their reactions, reading their body
language, and seeing their communication skills firsthand? And interviews are highly intuitive: most people are convinced they can tell a

great deal about a person from a short question and answer session. Scriven (1990) notes that interviews help reveal a candidate's level of grace under pressure, mastery of language, familiarity with current issues, knowledge of the hiring district, and a few intellectual qualities. "Much of teaching consists of presenting new material and explaining information to students," says Clement (2000, p. 26). "An interviewee who can thoroughly explain a grading scale to you can also explain it to students and parents."

Limitations of Interviews

Unlike classrooms, interviews are small-group encounters. Interviews have different goals than classroom teaching, and the perceptions of the interviewer are not the same as students'. Interviews too often assess interviewing skills rather than teaching skills; if a meeting with a candidate results only in vague impressions rather than in clarifying objective evidence about his or her track record, then it is useless for selection purposes.

According to Scriven (1990), teachers should never be selected solely on the basis of an interview. Interviewing hazards include learning more about the interviewers than the candidates, placing a premium on the peak performer rather than the constant achiever, lending too much weight to "show" qualities unrelated to classroom teaching, and general unreliability.

The Screening Team should pay particular attention to interviewee preparedness, interviewer skill (such as the extent to which he or she probes difficult topics), physical conditions of the interview itself, and the power relationship—e.g., whether the candiate is being interviewed by a teacher, principal, or superintendent. Among other things, the Screening Team should

☞ Select and train multiple interviewers
☞ Interview candidates more than once
☞ Control interruptions, secure a pleasant setting, and watch the time to ensure optimal interviewing conditions
☞ Consider the benefits of group interviews (e.g., varied points of view)
☞ Use a mix of standard and personalized questions

Purpose of Selection Interviews

Selection interviews can help the Screening Team
☞ Determine candidate skill level
☞ Decide whether the applicant fits the job
☞ Compare candidates to each other
☞ Sell the district and school to the candidate
☞ Identify red flags
☞ Fill in applicant profile and information lacking in previous reviews

These tasks can actually conflict with each other: for example, the systematic and structured questions necessary to assess knowledge, skills, and attitudes can also threaten the interviewer's ability to foster positive feelings and promote the district.

Structured Interviews

During structured or situational interviews, interviewees recall or hypothesize about specific behaviors and wrestle with job-related dilemmas, and interviewers base their conclusions on behaviorally descriptive scoring guides. Interviewers should

- ☛ Base questions on the specific knowledge, skills, and abilities necessary for the open position, with a focus on teacher behaviors
- ☛ Concentrate on district goals, programs, and themes
- ☛ Make objective decisions
- ☛ Be held accountable to the Screening Team, which should review and assess interview performance

Researchers find that predictive validity, consistency, and inter-rater reliability are all substantially increased by structured interviews (Harris & Eder, 1999). Still, many interviewers resist these types of interviews, either because they fear losing control over the process, prefer informal interactions, rely overmuch on gut feelings, or resent the time demands of training and accountability.

Principles of Effective Interviews

The Screening Team should only interview a small group of the most qualified applicants; interviewers should be carefully selected and trained, and should show evidence of genuine involvement with candidates. They need to be both tough minded and sensitive to the candidate's anxiety, while remaining assertive and maintaining control of the agenda. Good interviewers must know when to ask direct questions and when to subtly coax the answers out, as well as the difference between interrogating and following up. Interviewers should see each session as reflective of their own reputations and techniques.

The best interview programs include two to three individual interviews, followed by one group session in which both administrators and teachers ask questions of the candidate. The group session should include a mix of interviewers who have already reviewed the applicant's resume and some who haven't.

Types of Interview Questions

There are many different types of interview questions:

- ☞ Individual vs. sequential
- ☞ Closed (short answer) vs. open (extended answer)
- ☞ Standard (asked of all) vs. custom (candidate-specific)
- ☞ Easy vs. difficult
- ☞ Trait-based vs. behavior-based
- ☞ Competency-based vs. opinion-based
- ☞ Situational vs. principle-based
- ☞ Factual vs. hypothetical

The following four types are especially important to hirers:

- ☞ **Past-performance questions.** *Used to:* Solicit detailed examples of past performance.
- ☞ **Balancing questions.** *Used to:* Balance negative or positive responses with opposites (e.g., "what about a time when things did not go so well?" "Tell me about a success in that area").
- ☞ **Negative confirmations.** *Used to:* Solicit a second example to confirm a negative impression.
- ☞ **Reflexive statements.** *Used to:* Guide the pace and direction of the questioning (e.g., "I think it's time to move on, don't you?").
- ☞ **Reflexive mirroring statements.** *Used to:* Clarify what has been said (e.g., "So your opinion is that . . .").
- ☞ **Half-right reflexive questions.** *Used to:* Assess candidate's ability to speak own mind (e.g., "I've always thought that teachers should never negotiate with students about assignments or topics. Do you agree?").

Approximately 70 percent of the interviewer's questions should be competency-based and should focus on tangible instructional skills (e.g., how to begin a lesson), professional knowledge (e.g., copyright laws), classroom behavior (e.g., pacing classroom instruction), and interpersonal skills (e.g., dealing with a difficult parent). In addition, questions should concentrate on candidate behavior, either by describing past actions or discussing a hypothetical situation. Here's an example of behavioral and nonbehavioral answers to an interview question:

Q: Tell me about the time you realized that certain students consistently finished their work ahead of the rest of the class.

Nonbehavioral answer: I think it is very important to keep all students busy. Many discipline problems begin with idle time. My cooperating teacher said that "sponge activities" are very effective. Another common problem is that teachers do not know their students, and are surprised by uneven finishing times, which actually are very common and should be planned for. Also, seatwork needs to be demanding enough that even the fastest finishers should be challenged.

Behavioral answer: I asked individual students to tell me about what finishing early was like, and what it meant to them. I asked another teacher for her advice about dealing with early finishers. I changed my learning centers so that students could actually record their own progress while there. Lastly, I produced some study guides that allow students to start on their own work without my guidance. This student self control worked very well for about three-quarters of my students.

Assignment Questions

Prior to the interview, the Screening Team should ask the candidate to visit the hiring school, community, or Web site. The interviewer should then ask "assignment questions" related to the visits, such as "You were asked to visit our computer center. How would you use this resource?" or "You attended Science/Math Night. How would you have your students participate?" Additional assignments might include readings, visits to neighborhood parks or libraries, and attendance at school board meetings or parent nights. The Screening Team might also consider assigning tasks to applicants for post-interview reporting, perhaps asking them to submit a brief written reaction to aspects of the school program.

Types of Questions to Avoid

The following kinds of questions should be kept to a minimum:

- ☛ Leading questions (e.g., "We're under great pressure right now to raise test scores; how do you feel about testing?")
- ☛ Loaded questions (e.g., "So which is better, over-testing or over individualizing?")
- ☛ Trait questions that merely solicit candidate opinions, preferences, and self descriptions (e.g., "Describe your strengths." "How do you feel about whole-language approaches?" "Are you committed to teaching?")

Interviewers should also refrain from asking multiple-choice or true-false questions because they are either too complex to be easily understood or too limited for substantive answers. See Figure 4.1 for a sample list of questions not to ask.

Hirers should avoid conducting personality-profile and stress interviews. The goal of personality-profile interviews is to ascertain the applicant's character traits—making them very limited, because

4.1
Off-Limits Interview Questions

☞ How old are you?
☞ What is your race?
☞ Of what country are you a citizen?
☞ Tell me about your accent.
☞ How tall are you?
☞ What is your native language?
☞ How did you acquire your second language?
☞ What is your marital status?
☞ Are you a single parent?
☞ What is your preferred form of address: Miss, Mrs., or Ms.?
☞ What are the names of your next of kin?
☞ How many children do you have?
☞ What are your child-care arrangements?
☞ Do you own or rent your home?
☞ Do you live alone?
☞ Do you have any large debts?
☞ Who is your emergency contact?
☞ What is your sexual orientation?
☞ Tell me about your religious beliefs?
☞ Describe your political beliefs or affiliations.
☞ Describe your attitude toward unions.
☞ Of what clubs are you a member?
☞ To what organizations do you donate money or time?
☞ Are you physically fit?
☞ Are you disabled? If so, how severe is your disability?
☞ Have you ever been treated for any conditions or diseases?
☞ Do you use alcohol or drugs on your own personal time? Have you ever had a problem with either?
☞ What is your military service history?
☞ Have you ever been arrested?
☞ Do you have additional outside income?
☞ What are your retirement plans?

no single kind of personality is better for teaching than any other. Meanwhile, the conditions and goals of stress interviews—in which pressure is purposely applied to see how well the applicant can handle it—are so different from those of teaching that they too should be ruled out.

Combinations of Question Types

Interviewers might want to ask different types of questions in succession. For example:

Question 1: training and experience. "What preparation have you had for working with parents?"

Question 2: behavioral. "What steps did you take when a parent said, 'I am interested in better supporting my daughter in school'?"

Question 3: willingness to work. "How do you intend to develop your skills for working with parents?" "What evidence is there that you are a hard worker?"

Question 4: transitional. "Is there anything else I should know about your work with parents?"

For additional examples of question combinations, see Figure 4.2.

Organizing and Scheduling Questions

The Screening Team might consider the following guidelines for establishing interview question types:

4.2
Three Examples of Combined Question Types

EXAMPLE 1
Question 1: conceptual/theoretical. "What is an important skill for 2nd grade students?"
Question 2: past behavioral example. "How did you teach this skill?"
Question 3: analytical. "What were the results?"

EXAMPLE 2
Question 1: conceptual/theoretical. "What is your position on cooperative learning?"
Question 2: past behavioral example. "Give me an example of how you accomplished this."
Question 3: analytical. "How did cooperative learning add to student learning?"

EXAMPLE 3
Question 1: conceptual/theoretical. "Should schools teach character building?"
Question 2: past behavioral example. "Can you recall an occasion when you taught character-building skills?"
Question 3: analytical. "Was this time well spent?"

☞ Seventy percent of all questions should be highly structured. Of these,

- Five percent should encompass rapport building
- Five percent should be introductory
- Eighty percent should constitute core questions
- Five percent should address data confirmation

☞ The other 30 percent should include a combination of open-ended, hypothetical, and probing—i.e., clarifying and verifying—questions.

Selection interviews are not just about finding the best candidate, but also about whether or not the candidate wants the job. There is always a degree of tension to interviews; after all, interviewees are inevitably as concerned with trying to look their best as interviewers are with finding their weak spots. Consequently, hirers should do their best to make the interviewees feel at home, and should make encouraging remarks halfway through the session, such as "This is going well" or "This is good—I'm getting the information I need." Although physical attractiveness should never be taken into account during selection, studies show that it can be an overwhelming factor in human judgment.

How to Interview Well

For a successful candidate, the hiring interview is the beginning of a long relationship; favorable first impressions, therefore, are crucial. It is up to the interviewer to set a good tone from the outset. To ensure as smooth a session as possible, interviewers should attend to the following key points:

Preparation

- Seek their own interview styles rather than use someone else's.
- Practice interviewing techniques on several of the best teachers in the district.
- Create a thoughtful invitation to the interview, including
  - Maps
  - A preview of what to expect
  - Information about the district
  - Time and expected duration of interview
  - Names and duties of interviewers

- ☞ The URL of an Internet map site (e.g.,
  http://www.mapquest.com)
- ☞ A positive personal note to the candidate
- ☞ Consider the interviewing environment—it should be
  private, accommodating, and brook no interruptions.
- ☞ Make sure chairs are comfortable and don't wobble, and that
  the candidate is not facing direct sunlight.
- ☞ Know what topics not to ask about (e.g., age, marital status,
  religion).

A Good Beginning

- ☞ Present themselves appropriately: because first impressions
  never change, interviewers should strive to appear cheerful,
  comfortable, eager, and prepared.
- ☞ Have necessary materials—files, pencils, forms—on hand.
- ☞ Avoid scanning applicants from head to toe upon first meet-
  ing them.
- ☞ Give candidates a chance to catch their breath—provide
  them with water, juice, or coffee.
- ☞ Provide a brief tour of the school.
- ☞ Build rapport by asking about name preferences and engag-
  ing in small talk.
- ☞ Describe the purpose of the interview; emphasize that it is
  mutually beneficial.
- ☞ Separate interview data from prior paper reviews.
- ☞ Begin with familiar topics, such as the weather or an event
  going on at the school.
- ☞ Open with unthreatening questions to set the interviewee at
  ease; begin with an icebreaker question (e.g., "Did you have
  any trouble finding the school").

Listening and Questioning

- ☛ Pay attention to the power-relationship differences between themselves and the candidates (e.g., discuss their own past experiences as interviewees).
- ☛ Take charge of the interview, rather than wait to be influenced by the candidate.
- ☛ Always keep the goal of the interview in mind: to assess the candidate, sell the position, and verify information.
- ☛ Avoid winging it or basing judgments on gut reactions.
- ☛ Present a positive but accurate view of the position and district.
- ☛ Provide some elements of surprise (e.g., "You are licensed for high-school teaching; what would you do if we assigned you to kindergarten for a month?")
- ☛ Maintain eye contact with the candidate.
- ☛ Allow the candidate to answer questions as fully as possible; do not interrupt.
- ☛ Explain why they take notes and ask certain questions.
- ☛ Record first and overall impressions.
- ☛ Let their immediate emotional reactions to answers diminish, lest they judge the applicant too hastily.
- ☛ Define esoteric terms.
- ☛ Avoid comparing candidates to each other.
- ☛ Ask spontaneous, unscripted questions when deemed appropriate.
- ☛ Frame questions in simple language and divided according to topic.
- ☛ Probe their own areas of expertise heavily.
- ☛ Work methodically and stick to the interview plan.
- ☛ Estimate the candidate's capacity to grow into desirable characteristics.

- ☞ Use the 20/80 rule: talk 20 percent of the time, listen 80 percent.
- ☞ Encourage candidates to teach them new things about their areas of expertise.
- ☞ Pay attention to body language: lean forward, smile, maintain an open posture.
- ☞ Never register surprise or disapproval at a candidate's answers.
- ☞ Employ active listening. As Arthur (1998) and Messmer (1998) suggest, interviewers should:
  - ☞ Periodically summarize what they have learned from the applicant.
  - ☞ Filter out distractions.
  - ☞ Base new questions on newly supplied info.
  - ☞ Think faster than they talk.
  - ☞ Listen for connecting themes and ideas.
- ☞ When closing the interview, thank the applicant, inform him or her of the next steps in the selection process, and take care to end on a supportive note.

See Appendix C for a step-by-step list of possible interview questions broken down by category.

Avoiding Interviewer Bias

The very expertise necessary of all good interviewers—informed, expert subjectivity—can sometimes cross the line into prejudicial bias. Five specific kinds of bias in particular operate during interviews. These are based on

- ☞ Information about the candidate gleaned prior to the interview

- First impressions of the candidate
- A single statement or answer that may skew interviewer reactions to unrelated responses
- Nonverbal communication
- The interviewer's own experience or preferences

Additionally, Klinvex, O'Connell, and Klinvex (1999) suggest that hirers watch for biases due to

- Leading questions
- Personal or professional similarities between interviewer and candidate
- The "halo effect" of one or two outstanding applicant characteristics
- Pressure to fill the position
- Discriminatory information, such as age or ethnicity

One good strategy for overcoming bias is the multiple-interviewer session, as the variety of viewpoints helps keep subjective reactions to a reasonable level. I recommend that the final three candidates complete a total of two or three individual interviews and one or two group interviews.

Note Taking

Hirers should document all interviews by taking notes. These should include the reasons for the applicant's ultimate assessment, along with direct quotes from the candidate. Notes should refer to job-related issues only. Excessive note taking, however, can be distracting. And while some people feel that using numerical rating scales in their written records adds objectivity, the fact is that numbers on their own add little to no objectivity; the scale itself is subjective.

Common Interviewee Behaviors

Some candidates are skilled at creating a sense of ease and competence by talking or acting in a certain way. While this is pleasant, it has nothing to do with quality teaching, and interviewers should be careful not to be swept up by the applicant's charm. Other candidates are especially good at complementing the interviewer's manner: if the interviewers are aggressive, they become passive, and vice versa. This behavior creates a false impression of compatibility, which, again, is separate from teaching ability and should be treated as such. Other common interviewee behaviors include

- Self-enhancement (e.g., "I was exceptional")
- Other-enhancement (e.g., "you're the kind of principal I'd like to work for")
- Conformity of opinion (e.g., "I agree that a small district like yours is best for students")
- Justification of dubious qualifications (e.g., "student gains weren't measured, but our spirit was the highest!")

Dealing with Difficult Interviewees

Interviewers should be prepared to deal with difficult applicants patiently and courteously. If a candidate is especially shy or nervous, the interviewer might sooth him or her by adopting a softer tone, adjusting body language, and asking easy questions early on. Gentle acknowledgment of the discomfort can help. If the candidate gets flustered, the interviewer should intervene with statements like "that's alright, that seemed a bit different from what you intended. Let's go on to more important things."

Interviewers should periodically interrupt overly talkative candidates and steer them toward answering another question. Most overly dominating applicants can be controlled with direct but gentle statements such as, "Excuse me, we seem to have strayed," "It's important that we address certain questions," or "We really need to stick to our agenda and schedule." Especially aggressive candidates should be told explicitly to be more direct and provide shorter answers. In the most extreme cases, interviewers should begin talking along with the applicants until they are quiet. Interviewers should ask overly aggressive or emotional candidates what the problem is, and should let them know that interviews are not the best places to handle such issues. Some might offer a cooling-off period before trying the interview again.

Interviewer Training

Interviewers need to be trained. Some researchers suggest that training should include information on using rating scales and practice simulations (Palmer, Campion, & Green, 1999). Some other important training topics include

- ☞ Long-term district planning
- ☞ Ideas associated with the sociology of hiring
- ☞ Sequenced question strategies, types, and purposes
- ☞ Hiring law, including improper questions
- ☞ Types of decision making—e.g., unanimous vs. majority opinions
- ☞ The limits of interview data
- ☞ Use of interview data in combination with other sources

Potential interviewers should also sit in on interviews by the district's best veteran interviewers, or practice their interview techniques on district teachers. Trainers can even grade interviewers on their responses to simulated interviews (live or on videotape). Successful interview training should take around 20 hours to complete.

Interviewer Accountability

Some research suggests that interviewers are more consistent and accurate when they are held accountable for their judgments. To this end, the Screening Team should ask interviewers to draw specific connections between their observations and judgments, which the Screening Team can then analyze for logic, lack of bias, compliance with expected procedures, and agreement with other interviewers. Follow-up discussions with successful candidates are another way for the Screening Team to assess interviewers.

Group Interviews

Group interviews allow candidates to interact with several judges, and help district staff to feel involved and respected for their roles. Other benefits include

- Multiple areas of specialization among the interviewers
- The greater legitimacy of a group assessment
- Fuller recall and more comprehensive records of interview
- Reduction of individual bias through consensus
- Opportunity for members to challenge each other's observations, assumptions, and decisions

Of course, there are disadvantages as well, such as

- Greater risk of a breach in confidentiality
- Selection of additional personnel can be time-consuming and difficult
- Time demands of additional training, materials preparation, and deliberation
- Tension between teachers recognized as good selectors and those who aren't

☛ The increased likelihood of minority opinions and subsequent ill will

☛ Risk of turning off applicants if interviewers don't see eye to eye

Group interviewers should be chosen from the Screening Team, and should represent a mosaic of roles—e.g., teachers, administrators, parents, older students, staff. While involving parents and students can take time, it's well worth the effort and helps enrich hiring decisions (Fischer, 1981). The group interviewers should not include interviewers and paper screeners from earlier in the process. The district may want to include people who are not on the Screening Team as group interviewers. These people would not handle the paper screening or have a say in selection policy and final decision making. Such a separation of duties permits those who are not on the Screening Team to conduct other important tasks, such as follow-up phone calls.

Group interviews are best when the Screening Team draws up a printed protocol, which should include information on the interview setting, an agenda of questions, a list of prohibited topics, and a breakdown of interviewer roles. The interviewers should number between three and five, with one selected by the rest as a leader. An odd number of interviewers rules out split decisions. An agreed-upon core set of questions should be divided up among the interviewers, each of whom should be allowed a given number of follow-up and spontaneous questions. The group should agree on each member's roles ahead of time, as well; for example, one member might ask about subject matter while another concentrates on training and expertise. Questions may be asked in rounds, so that every line of questioning is heard, and seats should be arranged in an arc.

The Durham County School District in North Carolina uses a particularly unusual group-interview technique. Early applicant screening includes an "interview seminar" during which 12 to 16 candidates are interviewed at one time by a team of three district administrators. This procedure is perhaps not as personalized or as tailored to the individual candidates as others, but it does allow for discussions of the district, a somewhat collegial setting, disclosure of some teacher leadership qualities, comparisons between candidates, and efficiency. Following the seminar, some applicants are interviewed individually.

Teacher Perceiver Interviews

Some authorities on teacher hiring recommend psychological testing of candidates, often using the Selection Research Teacher Perceiver scale, a 60-item survey. The questions are arranged according to domains: Mission, Focus, Gestalt, Rapport, Drive, Empathy, Individualized Perception, Listening, Innovation, and Investment. Advocates of this type of test cite the low cost, ease of administration, and consistency across situations (Muller, 1978). However, researchers have concluded that the empirical base for such claims is weak; that the tests are only partially predictive of student ratings of new teachers, but not of improved student achievement or attitudes; and that the tests raise questions of conflict of interest for teachers with different favorite instructional approaches (Haefele, 1978; Miller, 1977; Yoder, 1976). Although the validity of this test has yet to be proved, Wise, Darling-Hammond, and Berry (1988) reported that many of the districts they studied used variations on this instrument.

Other districts use a standard battery of questions, either in interviews or on a survey, that are scored to yield applicant diagnoses according to different categories (e.g., "Personal Motivation," "Child-Centeredness," or "Preference for Collaboration"). Answers to these questions will often suggest candidate personality types. There is no research to suggest that any single personality type is best for teachers, but district personnel often prefer to work with people who think or act like they do. However, this attitude may be the opposite of what we need for healthy educational organizations, since schools must teach to a variety of student styles and preferences. It is up to each district whether to use personality profiles.

5

THE FINAL DECISION AND FOLLOW-UP

The district superintendent should usually make the final hiring decision; however, in a district where the superintendent has numerous other responsibilities, the hiring decision may be made by a person or team members who are charged with hiring in their job descriptions, who have been trained to hire, who are licensed to hire as part of their job, and who are monitored in their hiring practice.

Immediate Follow-up of Applicants

The Screening Team should alert the finalists of its decision, obtain a signed contract and personal commitment from the chosen candidate, and archive all applicant files for one year.

For Those Selected

Contact the successful candidate first by phone, with an immediate verbal offer, and then with a follow-up letter to confirm the decision and provide the applicant with contacts in case of any questions. The Screening Team should set a definite deadline for the candidate's final decision; three days is reasonable. If the applicant doesn't meet the deadline, the Screening Team should renew its search; if he or she does meet the deadline, the next step is to formally confirm the conditions of employment in writing.

The hirers should remain calm at all times and put the district's best face forward. They should not, however, make extravagant promises, oversell the district, or wait beyond three days for a decision.

If the top candidate decides not to take the job, it is important that the Screening Team not let the other applicants know that they weren't the first choice; in order to minimize gossip and prejudicial views about the new hire, hirers should not divulge too much information about the strength of the competition or degree of consensus among interviewers. Finally, the new teacher should be placed on district mailing lists, in order to become better acquainted with the new environment.

For Those Not Selected

Once the position has been filled, the hirers should notify the other candidates via mail or e-mail within one or two days, and definitely within 10 days of their last interview. The district is under no obligation to explain their decision. As Wendover (1998) says, districts ". . . are not obligated to explain [their] reasons for rejection and volunteering such information is just asking for trouble" (p. 177). It is virtually impossible to provide candidates with detailed assessments of their weaknesses, as well. Hirers should let rejected candidates know that they will be kept on file and contacted should a fitting position open up.

Applicant files should be kept for at least a year, but should then be destroyed to protect candidate privacy and conserve resources. The Screening Team should establish a specific protocol for document destruction.

Follow-up of New Hires

School districts can publicize their programs and teachers by issuing press releases when new teachers are hired. The selection Screening Team might also want to make a presentation in front of the school board, highlighting the new teacher's strengths.

New hires should receive their first paycheck before they start working. This is a show of good faith as well as an incentive to stay on board and can help to mitigate relocation costs for teachers.

Induction Programs

New hires should immediately be enrolled in an induction program, which could include staged orientations, financial support for moving and settling, inservice courses, visitors programs, and peer support groups. Good programs result in higher retention rates (Huling-Austin, 1987; Johnston, 1985; Peterson, 1990). An effective new teacher induction program should include

- Teachers at all levels, from beginners to veterans
- Carefully crafted building arrangements
- Smaller class sizes for beginning teachers
- Complete information technology support: access to consultants, computers, fax machines, telephones, and photocopiers
- Teacher mentors
- Multiple meetings scheduled throughout year, rather than one initial, all-purpose meeting
- Maps, handbooks, contacts, calendars, schedules, directories, evaluation forms, and a glossary of terms and programs
- Opportunities to visit other classrooms and resource centers
- Stress-management programs

Evaluating and Renewing the Hiring Program

In this step, the Screening Team should assess the efficacy of its selection system and prepare for the next round of hiring by

- ☞ Determining the best hirers on staff
- ☞ Interviewing the hired and the hirers
- ☞ Procuring the opinions of colleges and universities the applicant has attended
- ☞ Developing a hiring resources book

Process Validation

As Bolton (1973) has said, "correlations among . . . variables tend to change from time to time because both working conditions and personnel in schools change. Therefore, any measure of success of a selection process is likely to be only temporary, and the value of the procedure should be checked periodically" (p. 21). In other words, districts need to validate their procedures on an ongoing basis, and to alter them accordingly.

✓   ✓   ✓

As evidenced by the many different considerations discussed in this book, good teacher selection is as challenging as it is worthwhile. Hiring the best teachers is a school's best hope for quality education and depends on a few key principles:

- ☞ A large pool of applicants
- ☞ As much data as possible for every candidate
- ☞ Narrowing the pool in phases
- ☞ Involving staff in a variety of roles

If districts commit the time, effort, and resources necessary to put the guidelines offered in this book into practice, then they will meet their responsibility to employ the best teachers possible.

APPENDIX
A

ONLINE RESOURCES

General Hiring

HR-Guide. http://www.hr-guide.com/
!Trak-It Applicant Tracking System. http://www.trak-it.com/
 applicant_sbe.html

National Teacher, School, and District Registries

TeachWave. http://teachwave.com/
Project Connect. http://careers.soemadison.wisc.edu/projectconnect/
 mainmenu.cfm/

School Districts

Davis (Utah). http://www.davis.edu/
Miami-Dade County (Florida). http://www.dade.k12.fl.us/
New Haven Unified (California). http://www.nhusd.k12.ca.us/
Georgetown County (South Carolina). http://www.gcsd.k12.sc.us/

Boulder County (Colorado). http://bcn.boulder.co.us/univ_school/
Westport (Connecticut). http://teachers.westport.k12.ct.us/

Teacher Testing

Educational Testing Service. http://www.ets.org/
Graduate Record Examinations. http://www.gre.org/
National Board for Professional Teaching Standards.
    http://www.nbpts.org/

Education Policy

RAND Education. http://www.rand.org/edu_area/
National Center for Education Statistics. http://nces.ed.gov/
AACTE Education Policy Clearinghouse. http://www.edpolicy
    .org/index.shtml/

Education-Related Organizations

American Association of Colleges for Teacher Education.
    http://www.aacte.org/
Association of Independent Liberal Arts Colleges for Teacher
    Education. http://www.ailacte.org/
The Holmes Partnership. http://www.holmespartnership.org/
Council of Chief State School Officers. http://www.ccsso
    .org/intasc.html/
National Council for Accreditation of Teacher Education.
    http://www.ncate.org/
National School Boards Association. http://www.nsba.org/
National Association of Elementary School Principals.
    http://www.naesp.org/

National Association of Secondary School Principals.
    http://www.nassp.org/
American Association of School Personnel Administrators.
    http://www.aaspa.org/
American Council on the Teaching of Foreign Languages.
    http://www.actfl.org/
Mission of the Association for Childhood Education International.
    http://www.udel.edu/bateman/acei/
International Reading Association. http://www.reading.org/
National Association for the Education of Young Children.
    http://www.naeyc.org/
National Council for the Social Studies.
    http://www.socialstudies.org/
National Council of Teachers of Mathematics. http://www.nctm.org/
National Science Teachers Association. http://www.nsta.org/
American Federation of Teachers. http://www.aft.org/
National Education Association. http://www.nea.org/
National Board for Professional Teaching Standards.
    http://www.nbpts.org/

Teacher Evaluation

Teacher Evaluation: A Comprehensive Guide to New Directions
    and Practices. http://www.teacherevaluation.net/

Interviewing

The Gallup Organization: Perceiver Interviews.
    http://education.gallup.com/select/perceiverInterviews.asp

General Recruitment

Monster.com. http://occ.com/
Interbiznet. http://interbiznet.com/

Employment Law

The Alexander Hamilton Institute's Employment Law Resource
Center. http://www.ahipubs.net/reports/index.html/
The General Services Administration's Office of Civil Rights. http://
www.gsa.gov/eeo/

Minority Recruitment

NEA Guidelines for the Recruitment and Retention of Minority
Teachers. http://www.nea.org/recruit/minority/

APPENDIX

B

PARTICIPANT RIGHTS AND THE LAW IN TEACHER HIRING

Employment law is derived from the U.S. Constitution, federal and state statutes, state administrative rules, federal executive orders, and court cases. Each state has its own administrative rules and civil rights agencies; rulings in federal court cases apply directly to those states within the federal circuit of the case. Teacher selectors should follow district-hiring mandates and procedures as described in advertising, training, literature, and promises made at job fairs or interviews.

Teacher Hiring Bill of Rights

Each party during teacher selection has certain rights: applicants have a right to information on how to apply, for instance, and districts have a right to records of the candidate's past performance. Candidates do not, however, have a right to detailed analyses of their weaknesses and strengths. Figure B-1 presents a list of rights for school districts, applicants, and community members.

If candidates raise forbidden topics themselves, hirers should respond along the following lines before moving on:

B-1
A Bill of Rights for Teacher Hiring

Note: *The following declaration does not necessarily reflect state or federal law.*

During teacher selection, the school district has the right to
- ☛ Make personnel decisions intended to provide quality education
- ☛ Collect information relevant to its hiring role
- ☛ Act on such relevant information in the best interest of the students
- ☛ Expect candidate initiative in order to make the best decisions
- ☛ A thorough and rigorous evaluation of candidates
- ☛ Cooperative parents and teaching staff

Candidates have the right to
- ☛ Make their cases for employment at their own discretion
- ☛ Be judged by skilled selectors, according to the evidence provided, and only upon criteria related to job performance
- ☛ Know the general timeframe for review and deliberation
- ☛ Confidentiality and personal privacy
- ☛ Honor other professional commitments during the hiring process.
- ☛ Express unpopular views
- ☛ Refuse to engage in illegal acts
- ☛ Participate in union activities (except where limited by law)

The public, parents, and members of the community have the right to
- ☛ Expect children to be the paramount concern during the hiring process.
- ☛ Have their children taught by competent educators
- ☛ A fair and efficient hiring process
- ☛ Know the standards and criteria used for hiring
- ☛ A fair hearing of their complaints and concerns

- ☛ "That's an issue unrelated to hiring."
- ☛ "That's none of our concern—we certainly would never take that into account."
- ☛ "Excuse me, that's not a job-related kind of information."

☞ "That's a topic forbidden for consideration in hiring."
☞ "You've raised another issue that we have no right to ask.
I certainly will not take your statement into account or the
record. Pleases avoid that topic."

Fairness and Legal Principles

The following legal issues underlie the majority of hiring-related
lawsuits.

Discrimination. Unfair discrimination or disparate treatment based
upon race, color, national origin, gender, religion, age, certain disabilities, and (in some localities) sexual orientation. Discrimination may be
intentional or unintentional; intent may or may not be malicious.

Adverse systemic impact. The denial of equal-employment opportunities due to repetetive use of established, routine practices that do
not vary enough to enable all applicants and which narrowly create a
single path to employment.

Reasonable accommodation. Applicants with disabilities or religious
beliefs that do not inhibit work performance are entitled to reasonable accommodation thereof under the law. It is up to the applicants
to request accommodation and explain the nature of their disabilities
or beliefs to the district; both parties should then determine in good
faith whether the requested adjustment is possible. The district is
compelled by law to take affirmative steps to accommodate disabilities or religious practices, unless such action results in undue hardship
on normal operation of the school district. Applicants are not
required to divulge their disabilities or beliefs during the hiring
process, and the employer is not allowed to ask about them.

Negligent hiring. The failure to appropriately screen candidates who, once hired, violate the law.

Qualified privilege. The right of employers to share information about former employees, provided it is shared in good faith, with parties who have a legitimate need for the information, in response to specific questions related to work performance.

Defamation. The dissemination of false information that harms a person's reputation.

Negligent referral. The failure of candidates to divulge information that would otherwise have disqualified them for employment.

Reverse discrimination. Denial of equal employment opportunities due to unwarranted favoritism towards members of protected groups.

Ensuring the Legality of Hiring Practice

This discussion of legal issues is in no way a substitute for competent legal advice; unless they know what to expect from the law, educators can be paralyzed by fear of litigation. The law expects educators to use their professional knowledge and experience when hiring.

Seek competent legal advice. The Selection Committee should plan regular reviews, consultations, and training sessions with a lawyer. Hire a lawyer, preferably in state, who has represented aggrieved applicants in the past to review the entire hiring program and train the teacher selectors.

Keep applicant identities confidential. The Hiring Task Force and Selection Committee should only share candidate names with predetermined fellow hirers.

Verify all recruitment materials. In job announcements and flyers, be sure to mention that the district is an equal opportunity employer. Double-check all pledges and assertions for accuracy.

Do not enumerate too many specifics in job offer letters, lest they be perceived as conditions for employment.

Do not tell unsuccessful applicants why they were passed over.

Use applicant release forms. (See Chapter 1.)

Review the reviewers. Train teacher hirers about legal issues and evaluate them for quality, consistency, and compliance.

Evaluate your selection program. Hiring programs need to be habitually checked for bias, examined for unfair discrimination, and compared with other programs.

Train and evaluate all newly hired teachers.

Record Keeping

The Selection Committee should maintain comprehensive records of its practices and forms, as well as files on each candidate. Individual applications should be archived for about a year. In addition, the Committee should keep aggregate data about all applicants as a basis for future planning. Copies of work samples, portfolios, and videotapes should be destroyed after a year; requests for reasonable accommodation should be kept for two years, and immigration forms for three years.

APPENDIX

C

POSSIBLE INTERVIEW QUESTIONS

Opening/Ice-breaking

☛ How are you today?

☛ Tell me a little about yourself.

☛ Did you have any trouble finding our location?

☛ Do you feel ready for an interview?

☛ What are some of your most memorable experiences in education?

☛ Describe some strengths of your teacher preparation program.

☛ How do you recall your experiences as a student at the grade level and subject area for which you are applying?

☛ How did you find out about our district?

☛ What drew you to our district?

☛ What do you think of our school?

School Organization

☛ What has student teaching taught you about organizational and problem-solving options?

☛ What type and size teacher groups do you work best with?

☛ How would you describe good support from administrators?

☛ Define teacher collaboration and provide examples of your own practice.

☛ Tell me about your experience with difficult adults at school. How do you think schools should be set up to deal with these kinds of conflicts?

☛ Tell me about a situation where you had to convince a group, teacher, class, or administrator to change a procedure.

☛ What insights, if any, have you gleaned from alternative schools?

☛ What actions have you taken to better work with and understand school secretaries, janitors, and other staff members?

☛ What actions have you taken to better work with and understand school counselors, special educators, nurses, media specials reading specialists, and other support educators?

Knowledge of Students

☛ What have you learned about the developmental changes of students at different ages? Can you provide an example?

☛ How do you get to know (and know about) students?

☛ How do you get to know and use current student interests?

☛ How do you get to know about the different cultural back grounds of students?

☛ How do you keep in touch with youth culture outside of school?

☛ What do you find most challenging about the age you will be teaching?

Curriculum

☛ What should the curriculum content be for your grade or subject?

☞ Name two key ideas in your subject area.

☞ What do you find most challenging about the subject area you will be teaching?

☞ How should curriculum be determined?

☞ How do you incorporate subject-matter standards, career education, and reading, inquiry, and critical- and basic-skill instruction into your classes?

☞ What challenging subject-matter problem have you worked on lately?

Instruction

☞ Tell me some good ways to begin classes, lessons, or parts of the day.

☞ Tell me some good ways to end classes, lessons, or parts of the day.

☞ How do you feel about homework? Why?

☞ How do you alter instruction for students at different achievement levels?

☞ How do you teach for conceptual learning?

☞ How do you teach so that students remember what they have learned years later?

☞ How do you use planning in your teaching?

☞ Tell me about your ideas for grading and reporting progress to students and parents.

☞ Describe your use of tests.

☞ How do you feel about state- or district-wide standardized testing?

☞ How do you tailor testing for exceptional students?

☞ How do you handle controversial topics in the classroom?

☞ How do you incorporate computers and other technology into your classes?

☞ How do you incorporate textbooks into your classes?

☞ What experiences have you had with cross-age tutoring?

☞ Do you track your students' learning in previous and subsequent years? If so, how?

☞ What experiences have you had with reciprocal peer teaching?

☞ How do you set up cooperative learning in your classes?

☞ What are some good uses of field trips?

☞ Tell me about any unusual yet effective instructional techniques you have used.

☞ How do you use recesses or breaks as part of your teaching?

☞ How do you provide for students who are far more advanced than their peers?

☞ Describe your record-keeping systems.

☞ How should a teacher pass information about students along to the next year's teachers?

☞ What challenging teaching problem(s) have you worked on lately?

Classroom Management

☞ When is it appropriate to involve administrators in disciplining students?

☞ When is it appropriate to involve parents in disciplining students?

☞ What experience do you have with schoolwide discipline programs?

☞ Describe your philosophy of classroom management.

☞ How would you promote tolerance, acceptance, and cultural diversity in the classroom?

☛ How comfortable are you with classroom inclusion for special education, ESL, or culturally distinct students?

☛ Describe your experience working with teams on individual learning plans.

☛ How do you teach communication in the classroom?

☛ Describe your experience with class meetings.

☛ How would you handle unmotivated students?

☛ What challenging classroom-management problem(s) have you worked on lately?

☛ Describe a time when you lost control of your classroom.

☛ What role do you expect parents to play in classroom management?

☛ How would you use ground rules in your classroom?

☛ In your experience, how does classroom management differ at the beginning of the year from the rest of the year?

Other Classroom Issues

☛ What preparation or experience do you have working with classroom volunteers?

☛ How would you ensure gender-respectful treatment in the classroom?

☛ Describe your ideal classroom environment.

☛ What is your preferred method of arranging furniture and seating in the classroom, and why?

Dealing with Parents

☛ What are some ways in which you've kept parents informed about your class?

- What advice would you give to parents who want to support their children in the classroom?
- What preparation or experience do you have working with parents?
- Tell me about an experience you've had with a difficult parent.
- What experiences have you had with parent nights, class newsletters, e-mail communications to parents, or class Web sites?

Professional Life

- What level of support from or interaction with administrators do you expect from a school?
- How interested are you in teacher teams?
- Tell me about a time when you contributed to team building.
- What plans do you have for pursuing professional development as a teacher?
- How do you expect to contribute to your colleagues' professional development?
- How and where do you get ideas for your own professional development?
- Do you read regularly to support your teaching? If so, what do you read?
- What teaching ideas have you gleaned from professional magazines, journals, or organizations?
- Tell me about a work situation in which you have had to use fact-finding skills.
- What methods do you use to evaluate your instructional effectiveness?

☛ How do you feel about outside evaluations, such as student or parent surveys and peer reviews?

☛ Are you a member of any formal or informal teacher net works?

Educational Philosophy

☛ Describe the most effective teacher you have known.

☛ How should school systems respond to the achievement gap between rich and poor students?

☛ Respond to this statement: "Teacher should forget their training and start from scratch."

☛ Some people think that all students should be able to achieve certain standards, whereas others think that students should only be pushed as far as they can go. What is your position on this issue?

Personal

☛ Are you permitted by law to work in this country?

☛ Do you write or speak any foreign languages?

☛ Have you ever been convicted of a crime?

☛ What schools did you attend? Did you graduate?

☛ Do you wish to tell me of what teaching-relevant organizations you are a member?

☛ Describe your favorite professional problem-solving strategies.

☛ How can we help you to be the kind of teacher you want to be?

☛ What can you bring to this district that other candidates cannot?

- ☞ How do you manage stress?
- ☞ How do you manage conflicting demands?
- ☞ How well do you work with difficult adults and students?
- ☞ Describe your strengths and weaknesses as a teacher.
- ☞ How have you handled professional criticism in the past?
- ☞ How would you handle a meeting in which you couldn't get a word in, or where your words were misconstrued?
- ☞ If you were not a teacher, what would profession would you choose?
- ☞ What are the most striking differences between teaching and other jobs you have held?
- ☞ What do you find most difficult about teaching?
- ☞ Can you perform the tasks required of the position for which you have applied?

Assignment

You were asked to _____ [e.g., visit a classroom, park, or museum; read an article or book; watch a movie; listen to a tape].

- ☞ What did you notice during this activity?
- ☞ What aspects of the activity do you believe were handled well?
- ☞ What aspects of the activity do you believe were handled poorly?
- ☞ How would you have handled the activity, had you been in charge of it?
- ☞ How would a team of teachers have handled the activity?
- ☞ What kind of training would prepare someone to engage in this activity?

Ending

☞ How do you think this interview went?

☞ Did my questions cover everything you think is important?

☞ Do you have any reservations about accepting a job in this district?

☞ Is there anything that would prevent you from accepting this job if we offered it to you?

☞ Is there anything else I should know about you that has not come up in this interview?

BIBLIOGRAPHY

Al-Rubaiy, K. (1993). Five steps to better hiring. *Executive Educator, 15*(8), 21–22.

Anthony, R., & Head, S. (1991). *Interview training packet.* Evanston, IL: Association for School, College, and University Staffing.

Arthur, D. (1998). *Recruiting, interviewing, selecting, and orienting new employees* (3rd ed.). New York: American Management Associations.

Arvey, R. D. (1979). Unfair discrimination in the employment interview: Legal and psychological aspects. *Psychological Bulletin, 86,* 736–765.

Basom, M., Rush, R. T., & Machell, J. (1994). Preservice identification of talented teachers through nontraditional measures. *Teacher Education Quarterly, 21*(2), 47–57.

Beach, L. R. (1990). *Image theory: Decision making in personal and organizational contexts.* Chichester, England: John Wiley.

Bell, M. (1997). The development of expertise. *Journal of Physical Education, Recreation, and Dance, 68*(2), 34–38.

Berliner, D. (1994). *Implications of studies of expertise in pedagogy for teacher education and evaluation.* Paper presented at the 1988 Educational Testing Service Invitational Conference on New Directions for Teacher Assessment, New York.

Berry, B., & Hare, R. D. (1985). The dynamics of the teacher labor market in the Southeast. *High School Journal, 69,* 21–30.

Bird, T. (1989). The schoolteacher's portfolio: An essay on possibilities. In J. Millman & L. Darling-Hammond (Eds.), *The new handbook of teacher evaluation: Assessing elementary and secondary teachers* (pp. 241–256). Thousand Oaks, CA: Corwin Press.

Black, J. A., & English, F. W. (1986). *What they don't tell you in schools of education about school administration.* Lancaster, PA: Technomic Publishing.

Bolton, D. L. (1969). The effect of various information formats on teacher selection decisions. *American Educational Research Journal, 6,* 329–347.

Bolton, D. L. (1973). *Selection and evaluation of teachers*. Berkeley, CA: McCutchan Publishing.

Bridges, E. M. (1992). *The incompetent teacher* (2nd ed.). Philadelphia: Falmer.

Brooks, D. M. (1987). *Teacher induction: A new beginning*. Reston, VA: Association of Teacher Educators.

Brown, J. A. (1997, September). Avoiding employment law claims in the hiring process. *Victoria Business Magazine Online*. Available: http://www.viptx.net/vbm/.

Burnham, B. R. (1995). *Evaluating human resources, programs, and organizations*. Malabar, FL: Krieger Publishing Co.

Campbell, D. M., Cignetti, P. B., Melenyzer, B. J., Nettles, D. H., & Wyman, R. M. (1997). *How to develop a professional portfolio: A manual for teachers*. Boston: Allyn and Bacon.

Campion, M. A., Palmer, K. D., & Campion, J. E. (1997). A review of structure in the selection interview. *Personnel Psychology, 50*, 655–702.

Clement, M. C. (2000). *Building the best faculty: Strategies for hiring and supporting new teachers*. Lanham, MD: The Scarecrow Press, Inc.

Dailey, C. A. (1982). *Using the track record approach: The key to successful personnel selection*. New York: American Management Associations.

Dale, J. (1991). Leave hiring to the experts. *Executive Educator, 13*(4), 20–21.

Danielson, C. (1996). *Enhancing professional practice: A framework for teaching*. Alexandria, VA: Association for Supervision and Curriculum Development.

Danielson, C., & McGreal, T. L. (2000). *Teacher evaluation to enhance professional practice*. Alexandria, VA: Association for Supervision and Curriculum Development.

Deep, S., & Sussman, L. (1995). *Smart moves*. Reading, MA: Addison-Wesley.

Dipboye, R. L. (1992). *Selection interviews: Process perspectives*. Cincinnati, OH: SouthWestern.

Dipboye, R. L., Gaugler, B. B., & Hayes, T. L. (1990). *Differences among interviewers in the incremental validity of their judgments*. Paper presented at the annual meeting of the Society for Industrial and Organizational Psychology, Miami, FL.

Dipboye, R. L., & Jackson, S. L. (1999). Interviewer experience and expertise effects. In R. W. Eder & M. M. Harris (Eds.), *The employment interview handbook* (pp. 259–278). Thousand Oaks, CA: Sage Publications.

Dovidio, J., Kawakami, K., & Johnson, C. (1997). On the nature of prejudice: Automatic and controlled processes. *Journal of Experimental Social Psychology, 33*, 510–540.

Eder, R. W., & Harris, M. M. (Eds.). (1999). *The employment interview handbook*. Thousand Oaks, CA: Sage Publications.

Ferguson, J. E. (1983). Face to face: Making the best of the interview. *Teacher, 96*(2), 88, 90.

Ferguson, J. E. (1983). Interviewing teacher candidates: 100 questions to ask. *NASSP Bulletin, 67*(464), 118–120.

Fischer, N. A. (1981). Parents: Effective partners in faculty selection, hiring. *Phi Delta Kappan, 62*(6), 442.

Fitzgerald, P. (1970). Recruitment of teachers: A need for reevaluation. *Personnel Journal, 49*, 312–314.

Fry, R. (1996). *101 great answers to the toughest interview questions* (3rd ed.). Franklin Lakes, NJ: Career Press.

Fry, R. (2000). *Ask the right questions, hire the best people*. Franklin Lakes, NJ: Career Press.

Gatewood, R., Lahiff, J., Deter, R., & Hargrove, L. (1989). Effects of training on behaviors of the selection interview. *Journal of Business Communication, 26*, 17–31.

Gehrlein, T. M., Dipboye, R. L., & Shahani, C. (1993). Nontraditional validity calculations and differential interviewer experience: Implications for selection interviews. *Educational and Psychological Measurement, 52*, 457–469.

Gilliland, S. W. (1993). The perceived fairness of selection systems: An organizational justice perspective. *Academy of Management Review, 18*, 694–734.

Goodman, N. (1992). *Introduction to sociology*. New York: HarperCollins.

Graces, F. P. (1932). *The administration of American education*. New York: Macmillan.

Graves, L. M., & Karren, R. J. (1992). Interviewer decision processes and effectiveness: An experimental policy-capturing investigation. *Personnel Psychology, 45*, 313–340.

Graves, L. M., & Karren, R. J. (1996). The employee selection interview: A fresh look at an old problem. *Human Resource Management, 35*, 163–180.

Graves, L. M., & Karren, R. J. (1999). Are some interviewers better than others? In R. W. Eder & M. M. Harris (Eds.), *The employment interview handbook* (pp. 243–258). Thousand Oaks, CA: Sage Publications.

Gray, W., Nettles, M., Perna, L., & Edelin, K. (1999). The case for affirmative action in higher education. In A. Nettles & M. Nettles (Eds.), *Measuring up: Challenges minorities face in educational assessment* (pp. 167–194). Boston: Kluwer.

Griggs et al. v. Duke Power Company, 401 U.S. 424 (1971).

Haefele, D. L. (1978). The Teacher Perceiver interview: How valid? *Phi Delta Kappan, 59*(10), 683–684.

Half, R. (1985). *On hiring*. New York: Plume, New American Library.

Harris, M. M., & Eder, R. W. (1999). The state of employment interview practice. In R. W. Eder & M. M. Harris (Eds.), *The employment interview handbook* (pp. 369–398). Thousand Oaks, CA: Sage Publications.

Harris, M. M., & Fink, L. S. (1987). A field study of applicant reactions to employment opportunities: Does the recruiter make a difference? *Personnel Psychology, 40*, 765–784.

Herman, J. L. & Winters, L. (1994). Portfolio research: A slim collection. *Educational Leadership, 52*(2), 48–55.

Huffcutt, A. I., & Arthur, W. (1994). Hunter and Hunter revisited: Interview validity for entry-level jobs. *Journal of Applied Psychology, 79,* 184–190.

Huling-Austin, L. (1987). Teacher induction. In D. Brooks (Ed.), *Teacher induction: A new beginning.* Reston, VA: Association of Teacher Educators.

Interstate New Teacher Assessment and Support Consortium. (1992). *Model standards for beginning teacher licensing and development.* Washington, DC: Council of Chief State School Officers.

Johnson, S. M. (1990). *Teachers at work: Achieving success in our schools.* New York: Basic Books.

Johnston, J. M. (1985). Teacher induction: Problems, roles, and guidelines. In P. Burke & R. Heideman (Eds.), *Career-long teacher education* (pp. 194–222). Springfield, IL: Thomas.

Jones, D. E., & Sandidge, R. F. (1997). Recruiting and retaining teachers in urban schools. *Education and Urban Society, 29*(2), 197–203.

King, S. H. (1993). The limited presence of African-American teachers. *Review of Educational Research, 63,* 115–149.

Kinicki, A. J., Lockwood, C. A., Hom, P. A., & Griffeth, R. W. (1990). Interviewer predictions of applicant qualifications and interviewer validity: Aggregate and individual analyses. *Journal of Applied Psychology, 75,* 477–486.

Klinvex, K. C., O'Connell, M. S., & Klinvex, C. P. (1999). *Hiring great people.* New York: McGraw-Hill.

Lang, C. L. (1974). The teacher selection process in practice. In D. Gerwin (Ed.), *The employment of teachers.* Berkeley, CA: McCutchan Publishing.

Latham, G. P., & Sue-Chan, C. (1999). A meta-analysis of the situational interview: An enumerative review of reasons for its validity. *Canadian Psychology, 40,* 56–67.

Lavigna, R. J. (1996). Innovations in recruiting and hiring: Attracting the best and brightest to Wisconsin state government. *Public Personnel Management, 25*(4), 423.

Linn, M. (1998). When good intentions and subtle stereotypes clash: The complexity of selection decisions. *Educational Researcher, 27*(9), 15–16.

Maurer, S. D., Sue-Chan, C., & Latham, G. P. (1999). The situational interview. In R. W. Eder & M. M. Harris (Eds.), *The employment interview handbook* (pp. 159–177). Thousand Oaks, CA: Sage Publications.

McDaniel, M. A., Whetzel, D. L., Schmidt, F. L., & Maurer, S. D. (1994). The validity of employment interviews: A comprehensive review and meta-analysis. *Journal of Applied Psychology, 79,* 599–616.

Messmer, M. (1998). *The fast-forward MBA in hiring: Finding and keeping the best people.* New York: John Wiley & Sons, Inc.

Miller, J. D. (1977). *Preliminary investigation of the Teacher Perceiver instrument for teacher selection*. ERIC Document No. 206706.

Mitchell, T. R., & Beach, L. R. (1990). ". . . Do I love thee? Let me count . . .": Toward an understanding of intuitive and automatic decision making. *Organizational Behavior and Human Decision Processes, 47*, 1–20.

Mornell, P. (1998a). *Hiring smart: How to predict winners and losers in the incredibly expensive people-reading game*. Berkeley, CA: Ten Speed Press.

Mornell, P. (1998b, March). Zero-defect hiring. *Inc., 75–83*.

Muller, G. D. (1978). In defense of the Teacher Perceiver. *Phi Delta Kappan, 59*(10), 684–685.

National Board for Professional Teaching Standards. (1996). *What teachers should know and be able to do*. Arlington, VA: Author.

National Center for Education Statistics. (1997). *Credentials and tests in teacher hiring: What do districts require?* NCES Brief 97–592. Available: http://nces.ed.gov /pubs97/97592.html.

Norris, G., & Richburg, R. W. (1997). Hiring the best. *American School Board Journal, 184*(11), 46, 48, 55.

Palmer, D. K., Campion, M. A., & Green, P. C. (1999). Interviewing training for both applicant and interviewer. In R. W. Eder & M. M. Harris (Eds.), *The employment interview handbook* (pp. 337–351). Thousand Oaks, CA: Sage Publications.

Perry, N. C. (1981). New teachers: Do the 'best' get hired? *Phi Delta Kappan, 63*(2), 113–114.

Peterson, K. D. (1989). Assistance and assessment for beginning teachers. In J. Millman & L. Darling-Hammond (Eds.), *The new handbook of teacher evaluation: Assessing elementary and secondary school teachers* (pp. 104–115). Thousand Oaks, CA: Corwin Press.

Peterson, K. D. (2000). *Teacher evaluation: A comprehensive guide to new directions and practices* (2nd ed.). Thousand Oaks, CA: Corwin Press.

Peterson, K. D., Bennet, B., & Sherman, D. F. (1991). Themes of uncommonly successful teachers of at-risk students. *Urban Education, 26*, 176–194.

Peterson, K. D., Stevens, D., & Ponzio, R. (1998). Variable data sources in teacher evaluation. *Journal of Research and Development in Education, 31*(3), 123–132.

Pounder, D. G. (1989). Improving the predictive validity of teacher selection decisions: Lessons from teacher appraisal. *Journal of Personnel Evaluation in Education, 2*(2), 141–150.

Pulakis, E. D., Nee, M. T., & Kolmstetter, E. B. (1995, May). Effects of training and individual differences on interviewer rating accuracy. In E. B. Kolmstetter (Chair), *Interviewer and contextual factors that make a difference in interviewer validity*. Symposium conducted at the annual meeting of the Society for Industrial and Organizational Psychology. Orlando, FL.

Roehling, M. V., Campion, J. E., & Arvey, R. D. (1999). Unfair discrimination issues. In R. W. Eder & M. M. Harris (Eds.), *The employment interview handbook* (pp. 49–67). Thousand Oaks, CA: Sage Publications.

Rowley, D. J., Lujan, H. D., & Dolence, M. G. (1997). *Strategic change in colleges and universities*. San Francisco, CA: Jossey-Bass.

Sanders, W. L., & Horn, S. P. (1995a). Educational assessment reassessed: The usefulness of standardized and alternative measures of student achievement as indicators for the assessment of educational outcomes. *Educational Policy Analysis Archives, 3*(6).

Sanders, W. L., & Horn, S. P. (1995b). The Tennessee Value-Added Assessment System: Mixed model methodology in educational assessment. In A. J. Shinkfield & D. Stufflebeam (Eds.), *Teacher evaluation: Guide to effective practice* (pp. 337–350). Boston: Kluwer.

Sanders, W. L., & Horn, S. P. (1998). Research findings from the Tennessee Value-Added Assessment System database: Implications for educational evaluation and research. *Journal of Personnel Evaluation in Education, 12,* 247–256.

Schalock, H. D. (1979). Research on teacher selection. *Review of Research in Education, 7,* 389–417.

Schalock, H. D. (1998). Student progress in learning: Teacher responsibility, accountability, and reality. *Journal of Personnel Evaluation in Education, 12,* 237–246.

Schalock, H. D., Schalock, M. D., Cowart, B., & Myton, D. (1993). Extending teacher assessment beyond knowledge and skills: An emerging focus on teacher accomplishments. *Journal of Personnel Evaluation in Education, 7,* 105–133.

Schalock, H. D., Schalock, M. D., & Girod, G. (1997). Teacher work sample methodology as used at Western Oregon State College. In J. Millman (Ed.), *Grading teachers, grading schools*. Thousand Oaks, CA: Corwin Press.

Scheurich, J., & Young, M. (1998). In the United States of America, in both our souls and our sciences, we are avoiding white racism. *Educational Researcher, 27*(9), 27–32.

Schlecty, P. (1985). A framework for evaluating induction into teaching. *Journal of Teacher Education, 36,* 37–41.

Schmitt, N., & Chan, D. (1998). *Personnel selection: A theoretical approach*. Thousand Oaks, CA: Sage Publications.

Scriven, M. (1989). Teacher selection. In J. Millman & L. Darling-Hammond (Eds.), *The new handbook of teacher evaluation: Assessing elementary and secondary school teachers* (pp. 76–103). Thousand Oaks, CA: Corwin Press.

Scriven, M. (1994). The duties of the teacher. *Journal of Personnel Evaluation in Education, 8,* 151–184.

Snyder, J. (2001). The New Haven Unified School District: A teaching quality system for excellence and equity. *Journal of Personnel Evaluation in Education, 15,* 61–81.

Stanton, E. S. (1977). *Successful personnel recruiting and selection*. New York: American Management Association.

Streshly, W. A., & Grase, L. E. (1992). *Avoiding legal hassles: What school administrators really need to know.* Thousand Oaks, CA: Corwin Press.

Strike, K., & Bull, B. (1981). Fairness and the legal context of teacher evaluation. In J. Millman, (Ed.), *Handbook for teacher evaluation* (pp. 301–343). Beverly Hills, CA: Sage Publications.

Strike, K. A. (1989). The ethics of educational evaluation. In J. Millman and L. Darling-Hammond (Eds.), *The new handbook of teacher evaluation: Assessing elementary and secondary school teachers* (pp. 356–373). Thousand Oaks, CA: Corwin Press.

Tallerico, M. (2000). *Accessing the superintendency: The unwritten rules.* Thousand Oaks, CA: Corwin Press.

Tuller, W. L., & Kaiser, P. R. (1999). Using new technology. In R. W. Eder & M. M. Harris (Eds.), *The employment interview handbook* (pp. 279–292). Thousand Oaks, CA: Sage Publications.

Warner, C. (1994). *Promoting your school: Going beyond PR.* Thousand Oaks, CA: Corwin Press.

Weaver, W. T. (1979). In search of quality: The need for talent in teaching. *Phi Delta Kappan, 30.*

Wendover, R. W. (1998). *Smart hiring: The complete guide to finding and hiring the best employees* (2nd ed.). Naperville, IL: Sourcebooks, Inc.

Winter, P. A. (1996a). Applicant evaluations of formal position advertisements: The influence of sex, job message content, and information order. *Journal of Personnel Evaluation in Education, 10*(2), 105–116.

Winter, P. A. (1996b). Recruiting experienced educators: A model and a test. *Journal of Research and Development in Education, 29*(3), 163–171.

Wise, A. E., Darling-Hammond, L., & Berry, B. (1987a). *Effective teacher selection: From recruitment to retention.* R-3462-NIE/CSTP, January. Washington, DC: RAND Corporation.

Wise, A. E., Darling-Hammond, L., & Berry, B. (1987b). *Effective teacher selection: From recruitment to retention—Case studies.* N-2513-NIE/CSTP, January. Washington, DC: RAND Corporation.

Wise, A. E., Darling-Hammond, L., & Berry, B. (1988). Selecting teachers: The best, the known, and the persistent. *Educational Leadership, 45*(5), 82–85.

Wolf, K. (1991). The schoolteacher's portfolio: Issues in design, implementation, and evaluation. *Phi Delta Kappan, 73,* 129–136.

Wolf, K., Lichtenstein, G., & Stevenson, C. (1997). Portfolios in teacher evaluation. In J. H. Stronge (Ed.), *Evaluating teaching: A guide to current thinking and best practice* (pp. 193–214). Thousand Oaks, CA: Corwin Press.

Yate, M. (1994). *Hiring the best: A manager's guide to effective interviewing* (4th ed.). Holbrook, MA: Adams Media Corporation.

Yoder, W. H. (1976). A new approach in teacher selection. *Illinois School Research, 12*(2), 19–21.

I N D ε X

f indicates material appearing in a figure.

ABOUT THE AUTHOR

Kenneth D. Peterson is Professor of Education at Portland State University, Oregon. He has previously taught at the University of California, Berkeley and at the University of Utah. A former classroom teacher himself, Prof. Peterson has been teaching for 30 years, is on the editorial review board of the *Journal of Personnel Evaluation in Education,* and is president of the Consortium for Research in Educational Accountability and Teacher Evaluation (CREATE).

Prof. Peterson's other works include *Teacher Evaluation: A Comprehensive Guide to New Directions and Practices* (1995), a teacher-evaluation Web site (www.teacherevaluation.net), and over fifty journal articles on the subject of teacher quality. He can be reached at the School of Education, Portland State University, P.O. Box 751, Portland, OR 97207-0751.